GETTING UP, GETTING OVER, GETTING ON SERIES

Daily Meditations

For Surviving a Breakup, Separation or Divorce

Micki McWade, MSW

CHAMPI

WILLARD LIBRARY

D1490548

CHAMPION PRESS, LTD.
FOX POINT, WISCONSIN

Copyright © 2002 Micki McWade

All rights reserved.

No part of this book shall be reproduced, stored, or transmitted by any means
without written permission from the publisher. Although every precaution has
been taken in the preparation of this book, the publisher and author assume no
responsibility for errors or omissions. Neither is any liability assumed for
damages resulting from the use of the information contained herein. For more
information contact: Champion Press, Ltd., 500 West Bradley Road, A129, Fox
Point, WI 53217, www.championpress.com

Reasonable care has been taken in the preparation of the text to insure its
clarity and accuracy. The book is sold with the understanding that the author
and publisher are not engaged in rendering professional service.

The author and publisher specifically disclaim any liability, loss or risk,
personal or otherwise, which is incurred as a consequence, directly or
indirectly, of the use and application of any of the contents of this book.

ISBN 1-891400-32-0

Library of Congress Control Number 2002103110

Manufactured in the United States of America 10 9 8 7 6 5 4 3 2 1

Acknowledgments

The help of my editors, Brook Noel, Thelma Jurgrau and Sally Fay in preparing the manuscript has been invaluable. Brook believed in the project when she heard about it three years ago and has remained enthusiastic and actively supportive ever since. Her enthusiasm was contagious and I thank her.

Nicki Huebbe, a good friend and fellow social worker, has listened to and supported me whenever I needed a boost. Betty Ditlow read the manuscript in two days on a visit and further encouraged me.

Thanks are always in order to Elizabeth Sullivan, who helped me start the first Twelve Step Divorce Recovery Group and continues to be a support to me and the group. Also, my appreciation goes to all the group leaders and the women and men who have participated in that group for sharing their experience, strength and hope. Many of their voices will be heard in the meditations or quotes.

I want to acknowledge the writers of the quotes and thank them for the wisdom in their words. Where possible, the sources are listed in the back of the book. Many of these books are great reading while we recover and create new contexts for our lives.

I couldn't have done it without you all. Thanks so much!

Also by Micki McWade:

GETTING UP, GETTING OVER, GETTING ON:
A 12 STEP GUIDE TO DIVORCE RECOVERY

To Gary Ditlow

In appreciation of his love,
support and patience.

About this book...

The meditations are not in any particular order. The collection can be picked up at any time and started anywhere in the volume. Some will apply to you more than others, but if you keep an open mind and expand your thinking a bit, you may find something useful on every page. If you use this book for a second year, you'll see that the meditations apply differently than they did on first reading.

Some of the sources of the quotes are unknown to me. I am sorry about that and would be delighted to credit a source if I became aware of it. The quotations that have no attribution are mine in order to state some points I thought were important.

Introduction

A breakup of a significant relationship or divorce is one of life's most painful events. Those who haven't experienced it may minimize the depth of the hurt and sorrow we feel. They may expect us to move on in a couple of months and when we can't, imply we're emotionally inept. We may make similar demands on ourselves, expecting to heal in a given time period. We may feel disappointed or hopeless if we don't heal "on schedule." Why can't we just get over it?

It's both reassuring and demoralizing to understand that generally, for every five years of a marriage or serious relationship, it takes one year to heal. For some it will take longer and for others it will take less, but if people are telling you that after six months you should be all better, they are mistaken. Recovery takes time.

I was divorced in 1993, after 23 years of marriage and a three-year separation. I mourned. I hoped that I'd snap out of it—that I'd finally feel better, free and happy. Hadn't I suffered enough? I didn't snap out of it. A slow growth process happened instead. It required putting one foot in front of the other, one day at a time. I'd feel good some days and not on others. Gradually the good days outnumbered the bad but it took time.

My personal philosophy is that if I have to go through a difficult time, I might as well learn something in the process. One of the sources I learned the most from was a Twelve Step program. The Twelve Steps come from Alcoholics Anonymous and were written in the late 1930s. They have been in use ever since because they help those who are trying to change their lives. Many people have recognized the wisdom of the Steps and expanded their use to aid recovery in other areas, such as codependency and over-eating.

I learned about the Steps in Al-Anon, which is a program for families of alcoholics. There was a lot of alcoholism in and around my family. I joined that group to learn how to prevent handing down the disease to yet another generation, if possible.

Through Al-Anon I learned that I was powerless over other adults, and that by constantly focusing on others, I lost myself. I learned that a Higher Power is present, and that help and grace come from this Source. All I had to do was ask.

I learned to apologize, to accept situations I can't control as they are and to understand myself, including what makes me happy and what I can't tolerate. I learned humility and that I'm not always right; everyone has his or her point of view and is entitled to it. I learned that change is hard and that sometimes I need to ask for help to get there.

As I learned to apply these Steps to divorce, I wanted to share all this information with others because I found it so valuable. I also needed to keep myself on an even keel. I was raising four adolescent children when we separated and needed adult support. In 1993, I decided to start a Twelve Step Divorce Recovery Program because I wanted to move on and continue practicing the Steps with a group, but in a new context. I realized that although divorce papers were signed, sealed and delivered, I still needed recovery time. My ex-husband was going to remarry, and I knew the adjustment would be difficult for all of us.

I invited six friends to join me in a group setting like an Al-Anon meeting to talk about our breakup or divorce. Some friends were from Al-Anon and others had never heard of the Steps, but were interested in the work. Some were divorcing and others were coming out of a serious non-marital relationship. We've held Wednesday night meetings ever since and have had as many as 70 people at one time. More than 800 people have attended our meetings.

I felt compelled to share this program and adapted the Steps to divorce and relationship recovery. In March 1999 my first book, *Getting Up, Getting Over, Getting On: A Twelve Step Guide to Divorce Recovery* was published. It explains how the Steps can be used in this way and how to start a divorce support group. I am happy to guide anyone who wants to do that.

There is plenty of support for creating a hostile divorce. That is the norm today. Hostile breakups and divorces, however, lead to intense stress, possible dependence on drugs or alcohol, health problems, problems in the workplace, extraordinary expense and worst of all, difficulty and sadness for children.

The Steps are listed following the introduction and are referred to in some of the meditations. The Twelve Steps of Separation/Divorce Recovery are slightly different than those of AA. Both sets of Steps are included.

For the past four years I've sent an email "Thought of the Day" to group members. The thoughts are generally wise and uplifting quotations from various sources that provide inspiration, or food for thought. This book was born out of that tradition, and many of these thoughts are present in the following pages. I interpreted them to fit relationship-related issues and included an affirmation to make them directly usable. I encourage you to write your own affirmations to make the thoughts more directly applicable. In my recovery, I found it useful to start the day with a daily reading. The mornings were often difficult, but if I placed a positive thought in my mind early in the day, I felt stronger and more hopeful.

I read *The Language of Letting Go* by Melody Beattie, *The Courage to Change* distributed by Al-Anon, *The Woman's Book of Courage* by Sue Patton Theole and *Simple Abundance* by Sarah Ban Breathnach. These daily reading books were very helpful, and I looked forward to reading one or more each day, depending on my stage of recovery. They expanded my scope on a slow, steady basis and since my concentration span was minimal for a while, a page at a time was about all I could handle.

In addition, *The Seven Habits of Highly Effective People* by Stephen R. Covey and Tony Robbins' tape series, *Personal Power* were important tools for me. I recommend all of these to you, and there's a list of additional resources at the back of this book.

There are 365 meditations that span a year of recovery. My hope is that the ideas and long-range perspective will bring you some peace and a broader understanding of the situation as you move through the next 12 months.

There are references to divorce in this book but it was written in the hope that it will be useful for the end of non-marital relationships too. The word "separation" is used in a broader context than the pre-divorce period. A serious long-term partnership, whether hetero- or homosexual, leaves a deep wound that takes time to heal. When there are children involved, it takes longer.

There are certain principles in recovery from relationship that in my opinion are essential, and you'll see these themes repeated in different forms throughout the year. They include:

- Much of our quality of life comes from our choices and beliefs.
- If we do the best we can, day by day, we'll do well in time.
- A Higher Power is there for us, whether we believe it or not.
- What goes around comes around.
- Self-exploration is more important than a new relationship.
- Be as optimistic as possible.

My goals for this book are that it be used as a tool to aid and hasten your recovery and to offer an alternative thought system. Divorce is here to stay, but we can definitely improve our methods. If only one person in a couple chooses the high road, the other person will eventually be at least somewhat influenced by the integrity of his or her partner. If no one shows this consideration, problems escalate and everyone suffers in multitudes of ways.

I wish you the best in your recovery and on your journey. I hope that you will heal quickly, dream big and grow like crazy.

Blessings,
Micki McWade

TWELVE STEPS OF ALCOHOLICS ANONYMOUS

1. We admitted we were powerless over alcohol—that our lives had become unmanageable.

2. Came to believe that a Power greater than ourselves could restore us to sanity.

3. Made a decision to turn our will and our lives over to the care of God, *as we understood Him.*

4. Made a searching and fearless moral inventory of ourselves.

5. Admitted to God, to ourselves and to another human being the exact nature of our wrongs.

6. Were entirely ready to have God remove all these defects of character.

7. Humbly asked God to remove our shortcomings.

8. Made a list of all persons we had harmed and became willing to make amends to them all.

9. Made direct amends to such people wherever possible, except when to do so would injure them or others.

10. Continued to take personal inventory and when we were wrong promptly admitted it.

11. Sought through prayer and meditation to improve our conscious contact with God, *as we understood Him*; praying only for knowledge of God's will for us and the power to carry that out.

12. Having had a spiritual awakening as a result of these steps, we tried to carry this message to others and to practice these principles in all our affairs.

TWELVE STEPS OF DIVORCE RECOVERY

1. We admitted we were powerless over others, that our lives had become unmanageable.
2. Came to believe that a Power greater than ourselves could restore us to wholeness.
3. Made a decision to turn our will and our lives over to the care of God, as we understood God.
4. Made a searching and fearless moral inventory of ourselves.
5. Admitted to God, to ourselves and to another human being the exact nature of our failings.
6. Were entirely ready to have God remove our defects of character.
7. Humbly asked God to remove our shortcomings.
8. Made a list of all persons we had harmed and became willing to make amends to them all.
9. Made direct amends to such people wherever possible, except when to do so would injure them or others.
10. Continued to take personal inventory, and when we were wrong, promptly admitted it.
11. Sought through prayer and meditation to improve our conscious contact with God, as we understood God; praying only for knowledge of His will for us and the power to carry that out.
12. Having had a spiritual awakening as a result of these Steps, we tried to carry this message to others and to practice these principles in all our affairs.

The Twelve Steps are reprinted with permission of Alcoholics Anonymous WorldServices, Inc. Permission to reprint and adapt the Twelve Steps does not mean that A.A. has reviewed or approved the contents of this publication nor that A.A. agrees with the views expressed herein. A.A. is a program of recovery from alcoholism only—use of the Twelve Steps in connection with programs and activities which are patterned after A.A. but which address other problems, or in any other non-A.A. context, does not imply otherwise.

January 1

Vision is greater than baggage. —Stephen R. Covey

We may believe that our lives have always been hard, and we may also believe that, because of all that has happened to us, we may never succeed or be happy again. In other words, we may be in the habit of being unhappy or dissatisfied.

The wonderful truth is that we can decide to live differently from now on. We can choose to create a different life from the one we are leading now. If we hold a picture in our minds of what we want and keep that picture clear, we will create a new reality. We are not stuck in the past. We are not destined to repeat the old patterns if we choose not to. We create our future today and by making different choices now, the future will be different.

AFFIRMATION: Today I will create a mental picture of what I would like for myself in the future. I will think about that picture every day.

January 2

Imagine. —John Lennon

Creating a new life requires imagination. Making mental pictures is the first step in creating our new reality. Will our creation be by default, or will we make conscious decisions about how we would like our new life to be?

Teams training for the Olympics use visualization to envision winning results. We can use the same practice to foster growth and maximize potential in our lives.

Can we imagine a life of creativity and peace for ourselves? How about forgiveness for those who have hurt us? Can we imagine a full and happy life with our friends and family? How about wonderful work that satisfies us and makes us feel productive?

What will you imagine for yourself?

AFFIRMATION: Today I will begin to formulate a mental picture of how I would like my life to be. I'll write about it in a journal.

January 3

Our task now is not to fix blame for the past, but to fix the course for the future. —John F. Kennedy

Sorting out responsibility for what has happened in a relationship is an important part of recovery, and fixing blame seems to be necessary for a while but we don't want to get stuck at this stage. There are those who use the resulting anger as life-fuel and that may persist for years, resulting in poor mental and physical health.

As one who sailed, Kennedy knew that to get where he wanted to be he had to fix the course to arrive at his chosen destination. We have to do the same. Where do we choose to be in two years? In five years? How will we get there? What course shall we take?

Making those decisions is a far better use of time and energy for our own well-being than remaining in a state of anger and fixing blame.

AFFIRMATION: Today I will spend some time thinking about what type of life I want in the future.

January 4

We admitted we were powerless over others—that our lives had become unmanageable. —Step One of the Twelve Step Divorce Recovery Program

The biggest myth we create in our lives is that we have power over others. We can force issues in the short term, but not in the long run. We can't force someone to be who they are not. Many of us try so hard to make a person behave the way we'd like, we lose ourselves in the process. We forget to develop and take care of ourselves.

We can influence others by becoming a good example, but that's all. If you have tried to toilet train a two-year-old or control a teenager's driving habits, you know what I mean. We can set up limits and consequences, but we can't control behavior.

So what does that mean? We control *our own* behavior and development and take responsibility for *our own* decisions and actions. This is where our power lies. Let's learn to make use of it.

AFFIRMATION: Today I will examine one area in my life that has become unmanageable and think about ways to improve it.

January 5

Came to believe that a power greater than ourselves could restore us to wholeness. —Step Two

Separating from a partner creates a feeling of emotional amputation. A large part of our lives has been cut away, and whether or not the separation was our choice, healing is a painful undertaking. It takes a while to feel whole again.

One way to get to wholeness is to join a support group and practice the Steps. A lot of us consider a power greater than ourselves to be God or the Universe. Some consider the group a higher power because information is shared, friendships are made and the healing process is sped along by interaction with others. Many of us have our faith restored by practicing the Steps in the company of others.

Let's be open to information from sources outside ourselves. We read, talk things over, join a group, pray and meditate to feel whole again.

AFFIRMATION: Today I will be aware of a power greater than myself and begin to understand that I am not alone.

January 6

Made a decision to turn our will and our lives over to the care of God, as we understood God. —Step Three

What a relief this brings! We realize we are not alone and that we can ask and receive help and guidance with any of our problems. Lots of us think that this is the most difficult step because it requires letting go of complete control, but the irony is that we really have very limited control anyway.

In Step Three we learn to do the best we can and ask God to come along to guide us. We do our best and then turn the rest over to the care of God. The miracle of this Step is that when we are able to do it, the result is so much better than we ever imagined. The more we turn our worries over to God, the more results we'll see. As we recognize that prayers are answered, we'll ask for help more often. This is how faith grows.

We begin to realize that we are not alone. Our days go better, we become more lovable, more legitimate, more successful. This practice changes our lives.

One caution to keep in mind is that God changes us, not other people, for our own sake. God helps us heal, improve, understand, accept, grow, succeed, and make better decisions when we're willing. Because we have free will, we have to choose to accept God's help. When we pray for results in others, they too must be willing to accept it.

AFFIRMATION: Today I will ask for God's help with something I'm worried about and stay alert for the response.

January 7

I am an open and receptive vessel for Divine Abundance.
—Author's daily affirmation

When we practice Step Three—*Made a decision to turn our will and our lives over to the care of God, as we understood God*—we begin to see that God works in our lives in mysterious and wonderful ways.

It's possible that we don't ask for enough from God. We need to bring our Higher Power into all our problems, worries and needs. When we use an affirmation like this, we become open to all the gifts that are meant for us. Abundance includes many things: our precious children, financial security, having friends who care about us, having enough to eat, a place to live and a job we like. Let's be open to the gifts of God because they often include more than we may have imagined for ourselves.

AFFIRMATION: Today and for a few days, as an exercise, I will stand with my arms wide open and say to this affirmation. I will notice any change that occurs.

January 8

We'll write them down,
and put them in, she said,
those things we can't control,
those things that pain and puzzle us
and make us weep inside.
God can, especially when we can't.
Have faith that this will work. — Esther C.

In Step Three, we are asked to turn our will and our lives over to the care of God, as we understand God. The God Can Exercise is one way to practice this idea. We may have tried to resolve a problem many times without success. It's frustrating and sometimes frightening when we don't know what else to do. We may feel we have nowhere to turn.

The God Can is a container for these problems. Take a can and cut a slit in the lid. Label the container "God Can." When we need help with a problem, write it down on a slip of paper and place it in the container. What we can't do, God CAN—get it?

This exercise is used in divorce recovery groups to demonstrate turning a problem over to God: to give up control and symbolically place it in the hands of the Higher Power. In the weeks following this exercise, we have been amazed by the answers that have come. This has been true for believers and nonbelievers alike.

AFFIRMATION: Today I will make myself a God Can and when I feel overwhelmed, hopeless or frustrated, I'll put my request for help into it and ask God to take it.

January 9

Made a searching and fearless moral inventory of ourselves.
  —Step Four

We take an inventory of ourselves to understand more deeply who we are and what we need to change at this critical time. What are our strengths? Our weaknesses? We all have a number of both. What needs our attention? What can we rely on? What do we do well? What do we *like* to do? What makes us crazy, sad, sick? The more we know about our inner workings, the better chance we have of creating a satisfying life for ourselves. Therapy and trusted friends can help us answer these questions.

The Twelve Step program is a gentle one. Step Four does not suggest being hard on ourselves—only to understand how we can create a fulfilling life. An inventory suggests looking ourselves over and deciding what we like and what no longer works for us. We have an opportunity for reinvention.

AFFIRMATION: Today I will determine one strength and one weakness in myself, knowing awareness is the beginning of change.

January 10

If you want to know your past life, look at your present condition; if you want to know your future life, look at your present actions. —Buddhist teaching

This Buddhist precept correlates to Step Four: *Made a searching and fearless moral inventory of ourselves.* Until we do an assessment of where we are now, see where changes need to be made and are willing to make them, our past will repeat itself. At the end of a significant relationship, re-evaluation is necessary.

Let's ask ourselves "What am I doing now that stands in the way of the life I want? What am I doing right? What's not working? What can I change to make things work better?"

AFFIRMATION: Today I will notice my daily routine and determine if there is anything I am doing that will make my future life less than I want it to be.

January 11

Admitted to God, to ourselves and to another human being the exact nature of our failings. —Step Five

This Step further expands awareness. When we admit to God, we are forgiven. When we admit to ourselves, we become empowered because taking responsibility is the second step in correction. When we talk over our shortcomings with someone we trust, we realize we are human—no more, no less.

Obviously, practicing Steps Four and Five require much more than a day's work. They can be done alone by writing in a journal or at a meeting. In AA and Al-Anon, it's done with a sponsor—a supportive person who helps us learn how to change patterns of behavior through the practice of the Steps.

This Step is practiced to help us clarify what we need to improve. We do it with others to avoid being too hard on ourselves and to get some honest feedback.

AFFIRMATION: Today I will think about asking a person I trust to help me with my recovery.

January 12

Were entirely ready to have God remove our defects of character. —Step Six

To become *entirely* ready to give something up is different from saying "I think I'll stop procrastinating, be nicer to my children, give up smoking, lose weight, start exercising, get organized or go back to school, etc." It means "I am ready to do it *today*, and I'll do whatever it takes to get it done."

AFFIRMATION: Today I will ask my Higher Power to help me give up a behavior that I don't like.

January 13

When you flee temptations, don't leave a forwarding address.
—God's Little Devotional Book

If we want to stop smoking, we don't carry a pack of cigarettes. If we want to avoid calling our ex-partner, we don't leave his or her new number right in front of us. If we decide to diet, we better not buy those cookies at the store.

This quote is another way to think about Step Six: *Were entirely ready to have God remove our defects of character.* If we are really ready to stop a behavior, we won't leave an avenue open to make a U-turn back to the habit or behavior we want to change. If we leave that forwarding address, we aren't really ready to let it go.

AFFIRMATION: Today I will not sabotage myself for any reason.

January 14

Humbly asked God to remove our shortcomings. —Step Seven

Step Four is to recognize, Step Five is to admit, Step Six is to be ready to change and Step Seven is to realize that we need support in making those changes. Resistance to a new, healthy behavior sometimes creates a fog around what we want to change. We may ask "Is it really so bad?" "Do I really want to do this?" New behaviors may feel strange and unfamiliar. We will often feel a strong pull toward the old ways.

Asking God for help with transformation gives us the strength we need to be successful and adds a booster rocket to our intention. It's hard to change and to keep the improvement going until it becomes a new habit. Let's take all the help we can get!

AFFIRMATION: Today I will ask God to support my intention for improvement.

January 15

Made a list of all persons we had harmed and became willing to make amends to them all. —Step Eight

Step Eight is where we begin to work on our relationships. Most of us have guilt regarding something we did or failed to do to someone. Carrying that around weighs us down. Making this list organizes our thinking and allows us to examine issues more fully. We may see that we needn't feel badly about some of the items after all.

For those who require amends, we become willing to make things right. Often this requires only an apology, but sometimes it requires more. In this Step, only the list and willingness are necessary.

Many of us need to place ourselves on this list, because we may have tolerated too much and not protected or cared for ourselves as we might have.

AFFIRMATION: Today I will make a list of the people I have harmed by the things I've done and not done. I will put myself at the top of the list.

January 16

Made direct amends to such people wherever possible, except when to do so would injure them or others. —Step Nine

Step Nine requires that we put into action, wherever possible, the plan we made in practicing Step Eight. We apologize, forgive, pay back, return items, keep unkept promises. When a person is unreachable or deceased, we can write a letter stating what is in our heart. On some level, they will receive our message.

If we take this action with an expectation of return, we are not practicing Step Nine. We can only do our best to make things right from our perspective, and by doing so we eliminate the burden of guilt because we have made our amends with the best of intentions.

In practicing this Step, we must carefully evaluate how we plan to make amends. Consideration and compassion are essential.

AFFIRMATION: Today I will make an apology or keep a promise.

January 17

Continued to take personal inventory and when we were wrong, promptly admitted it. —Step Ten

To admit we were wrong when we made a mistake is a sign of character strength. Everyone makes mistakes and most of us do it often. It's part of being an imperfect human being. When we learn to apologize quickly for an error, we see that the incident is over. No guilt, no cover-up, we move on.

A strength that comes from practicing Step Ten is that we learn to take *our* personal inventory, not someone else's. This avoids all kinds of confusion and frustration. We develop our personal strength by improving ourselves, not by criticizing others.

AFFIRMATION: Today I will promptly apologize, if necessary, and feel the peace that comes from taking responsibility for my actions.

January 18

Where so many hours have been spent in convincing myself that I am right, is there not some reason to fear I may have been wrong?
—Jane Austen

Whenever we find ourselves rationalizing and obsessing over an issue or a disagreement, it may be because we haven't taken responsibility for our part. When we recognize and understand our contribution to the problem, it's easier to find peace and forgiveness. Step Ten suggests promptly admitting when we are wrong. A worthy goal is to get back to serenity as quickly as possible.

AFFIRMATION: Today I will contemplate my role in creating or perpetuating a problem. I will reason it out with someone else if necessary.

January 19

Sought through prayer and meditation to improve our conscious contact with God, as we understood God, praying only for knowledge of His will for us and the power to carry that out.
—Step Eleven

Prayer is asking, and meditation is listening. Most of us have been taught that God hears our prayers. The problem is that most of us don't take time to listen for the answer. When we ask God to come into our day and be with us, life begins to improve. So the more contact we have with God, the better. As a result, people react to us differently, we feel less harassed and things seem to go our way more often.

We may hesitate to ask what God's will is for us because we think we know exactly what would make us happy. The problem is that as human beings, we are very short-sighted. God has the big picture, and if we don't get what we pray for it's because something better is waiting for us.

AFFIRMATION: Today I will spend some quiet time in meditation and listen.

January 20

Having had a spiritual awakening as a result of these Steps, we tried to carry this message to others and to practice these principles in all our affairs. —Step Twelve

When we take the time to truly practice each Step—and it usually takes at least a year to put all of them to use in our lives—we wake up. We come to understand that a Higher Power is there for us, and that taking care of ourselves and our responsibilities is the way to serenity. We begin to use these principles in other areas of our lives and see that truth is truth. We teach by example, without saying a word.

When people ask us how we learned to be serene in the face of difficulty, we can tell them about the Steps and our practice.

AFFIRMATION: Today I will think about how the wisdom of the Steps may apply in other areas of my life.

January 21

Love and fear cannot exist in our hearts at the same time. Choose love—it feels much better.

We can't hold two opposing thoughts in the mind at the same time. It's up to us to choose which thoughts we'll entertain. While fear is a common feeling in divorce, we can choose to experience love. We can change our state of mind by taking a walk, doing some exercise, making a phone call, attending a meeting or church service, playing some music, playing with a pet. When we choose to stay in fear we shut down, eventually becoming paralyzed and depressed. We have to consciously and literally change our minds by doing something different. It may not seem like it works at first, but if we keep going, we'll feel a change.

AFFIRMATION: Today I will experiment with changing my frame of mind. I will search for an activity or a friend to help me.

January 22

Come to the edge,
Life said.
We are afraid,
They said.
They came,
It pushed
and
They flew. —Unknown

While living through divorce, it's natural to be afraid. So many major changes take place. Change, however, can push us to new heights that are undreamed of now.

Not only do circumstances change, but *we* are also transformed. It's up to us to create wonderful new things for ourselves—to learn to fly solo. For those who have been married for many years, being alone may seem bleak and lonely at first, *but* it's also an opportunity to explore our ideas and needs, and redefine our reality. Believe it or not, this may turn out to be a positive experience.

Many people who were devastated by their partner's leaving and have been on their own for a few years wouldn't choose to go back to their marriage. They have created a new sense of self and prefer life in the present to what it was in the past.

AFFIRMATION: Today I will have faith that I will be able to fly when necessary.

January 23

Love is a verb.

Most of us think of love as a thing—something we want to receive or give away. Instead, think of it as action. We feel unloved during divorce when people who formerly loved us pull away. This may include our spouse, in-laws and friends we had as a couple. We may feel abandoned and lonely.

To get back into the stream of love, do something loving. It can be for a stranger, a friend, an elderly person in a nursing home, a dog at the pound or a friend who is having a hard time. It may be a quick visit or a timely phone call to lend support, or just giving someone a hug. These seemingly small acts may have a profound effect on the receiver and will make us feel better too.

AFFIRMATION: Today I will do something loving for another being without expectation of return, and feel the joy that giving brings.

January 24

Keep walking though
There's no place to go.
Don't try to see through
the distances.
That's not for human beings.
Move within.
But don't move the way fear makes you move. —Jal al-din Rumi

Some days our goal is to keep moving. We may be so bogged down with worry and feelings of sadness that we want to stop, get into bed and pull up the covers—but because of commitments to others, we need to keep walking.

During divorce we try to determine how we can protect ourselves for the future, but it isn't possible to think of everything. It's much more important to keep relationships alive even if they have been transformed. Agreements are important, but more so is the execution of those agreements, which depends on the cooperation among all parties.

If we keep taking the high road, in time we'll see that we have arrived safe and sound.

AFFIRMATION: Today I will not let fear control my life. I'll take one day at a time.

January 25

Anger and hatred are our real enemies. These are the forces we most need to confront and defeat, not the temporary "enemies" who appear intermittently throughout life.
—His Holiness the Dalai Lama

Anger is a companion of divorce— a natural reaction to what is happening in our lives. Often we find the adjustments of the early stages to be harder than anticipated. Shifting from the familiar to the unfamiliar can cause discomfort, hurt and anger.

Hatred may be present too—at least for a while. We may feel extreme resentment toward others who are threatening life as we knew it. It's important to keep in mind that "this too shall pass," and not become mired in anger and hatred. These feelings rob us of joy and vitality, of creativity and productivity, and keep us stuck in the past. We need to realize that these states are our choice, and it is *our* lives that are affected—not those we hate. It is up to us to determine how long and how much we will allow any negative situation to take over our lives.

AFFIRMATION: For today I will decide how much I will allow negative feelings to control my state of mind.

January 26

Anger is like taking poison and expecting the other person to die.
—Rabbi Marc Gelman

We may feel very angry at times and have a very good reason to feel that way but the effect of that anger hurts *us* most of all. Sometimes anger is useful because it creates the energy to move forward or clarifies a muddy situation. To actively feed anger and keep it alive, however, creates ulcers, headaches and emotional chaos.

We may feel like we are punishing another by staying angry, but we affect ourselves most of all. We have to ask ourselves if it's worth it.

AFFIRMATION: Today I will look at the impact of my anger in my own life and reduce it where I can.

January 27

Live
never to be ashamed
if anything you do or say is published
around the world —
even if what is published —
is not true. — Richard Bach

Serenity, a goal of any Twelve Step program, can only be achieved by doing what is right, regardless of the inclination to do otherwise. If we do the right thing, we can rest on the knowledge that we did our best. If we live so we never have to be ashamed of what we have said or done, others will not even believe those negative statements. On the other hand, if we consistently lie, cheat, criticize, hoard or are unkind, accusations will be believed even if we are innocent of a particular wrongdoing.

We are recognized for who we are. It shows even if we try to hide our shortcomings. So much of what we know about one another is from our unconscious ability to read non-verbal cues. If we live like this quote suggests, we needn't worry about the impressions we make.

AFFIRMATION: Today I will evaluate what I do and say and begin to change what may be inappropriate.

January 28

Apology, like humility, is vastly underrated. Some think that to apologize is to admit weakness, but the opposite is actually true.

Guilt is wicked. It robs us of peace and keeps us awake at night. It's what makes us toss and turn with the "coulda-shoulda-woulda's." Divorce provides plenty of opportunities for guilt — what we do and say to our spouses, our children, our family and friends when we are upset, for example. We are upset and make mistakes because we are not operating at full capacity. Actually it's like trying to function while suffering with the flu. Mistakes happen more often under these circumstances.

We are human and make mistakes. No one is perfect or mistake-free. What keeps us from doing more damage is the ability to apologize rather than trying to cover up or make excuses. While it may be more difficult to do initially, it saves a great deal of angst in the long run. Apology reduces or removes guilt! When we apologize, it's over.

Some of us have to be careful of apologizing *too* much—for things we didn't create or that we had no responsibility for. Only we know whether we fall into the first or the second category.

AFFIRMATION: Today I will make an effort to apologize quickly where necessary and not carry the burden of guilt for my behavior.

January 29

No pessimist ever discovered the secrets of the stars, or sailed uncharted land, or opened a new heaven to the human spirit.
—Helen Keller

Because separation and divorce are so difficult, their positive aspects are often overlooked. The tumult, the necessary concern for the children, wrangling over property, legal fees and taking sides all have a front row seat, and that's all that is seen from the stage.

These are only half of the possibilities. Behind the front row, opportunities for growth abound. Change forces movement. We have the choice of fighting change or making conscious growth-producing decisons. Those who attempt to hold on to the past sign up for a life of frustration. Those who decide to make the best of things and be open to new experiences will create a great new life—regardless of age.

A pessimistic attitude stops growth and creates our own defeat.

AFFIRMATION: Today I will take one problem and find an opportunity in it—a way in which I can grow.

January 30

Kind words can be short and easy to speak, but their echoes are truly endless. —Mother Teresa

Separation and divorce may cause us to occasionally become self-absorbed. We can get stuck in our fear and sadness. One way to lighten our own depression is to find something nice to say about, or to someone else. A kind word can change someone's perspective and may be remembered for years.

By making another person happy, happiness spills over into us. Saying something nice to a child, to someone who is feeling low or to a co-worker who is doing a good job will lift that person and ourselves at the same time.

AFFIRMATION: Today I will say as many kind things as I can and observe how this action affects my own state.

January 31

Have no fear
of moving into the unknown.
Simply step out fearlessly
knowing that I am with you,
therefore no harm can befall you;
all is very, very well.
Do this in complete faith and confidence. —Eileen Cady

Ask your Higher Power to be with you today. When you ask, the Higher Power comes. There are many things that are unknown when we start off on the path of separation, and facing the unknown brings anxiety. Faith is knowing that we are not alone, which inspires our courage. As our faith grows by asking for help and guidance, our fear lessens. Ask your Higher Power to accompany you to the attorney's office and into other situations that may prove problematic. You will notice a difference in the general tone of what transpires.

Ask and you shall receive.

AFFIRMATION: Today I will ask my Higher Power to be with me, and I will stay alert to the internal changes this creates.

February 1

Life is eternal and love is immortal
and death is only a horizon.
Life is eternal as we move into the light
and the horizon is nothing
but the limits of our sight. —Carly Simon

If we look at life today from the perspective of the whole, we may see that while this period is very difficult, in the grand scheme of things it's manageable. Life goes on, love goes on. Change enters and reconfigures our lives but life still moves along and eventually becomes good again, and often becomes even better than we can imagine right now.

It's important not to limit ourselves by thinking "I could never do this...or that!" The horizon is nothing but the limits of our sight. Keep all possibilities open.

AFFIRMATION: Today I will become aware of how I limit myself.

February 2

We only want that which is given naturally to all people of the world, to be masters of our own fate, only of our fate, not of others, and in coop-eration and friendship with others. —Golda Meir

In property agreements, it's important to think in terms of sharing what is available rather than fighting over what is yours, mine and ours. The more we struggle, particularly with lawyers involved, the fewer resources we have left.

Whether we are in a relationship or not, we still want to be masters of our own fate while allowing others to be masters of theirs. If we can do this while maintaining important relation-ships—in cooperation and friendship with others—we will have fulfilling lives.

When we are parents, it's important to maintain mutual re-spect for each other because we will be connected through our children forever. The tie as a couple has not been broken, only re-configured.

AFFIRMATION: Today I will contemplate what it means to be the master of my own fate while being considerate of others.

February 3

Both abundance and lack exist simultaneously in our lives, as parallel realities. It is always our conscious choice which secret garden we will tend. When we choose not to focus on what is missing from our lives but are grateful for the abundance that's present—love, health, family, friends, work, the joys of nature and personal pursuits that bring us pleasure—the wasteland of illusion falls away and we experience heaven on earth.
    —Sarah Ban Breathnach

We manifest what we give attention to. If we think about the quality of our lives as always being difficult and lacking, that's what we will continue to experience. If, instead, we think thoughts that reflect plenty, we will create abundance.

Thought is very important and underestimated in its power. We undermine ourselves when we allow and encourage negative self-talk to rumble around in our minds. The type of thoughts we entertain is our choice—we can stay with the negative or literally direct our minds toward the positive. For example, rather than thinking "I'll never have enough money after this divorce!" think instead "There's plenty to go around and I'll be fine." Not only will you feel better immediately, but you'll be creating a different reality for the future.

AFFIRMATION: Today I will monitor my thinking to catch my negative thought processes and attempt to find a positive aspect to all the situations I encounter.

February 4

Between stimulus and response, man has the freedom to choose.
    —Viktor Frankl

When we are upset and agitated we commonly react too quickly. This statement reveals the importance of thinking before responding. Regardless of how we are provoked, we are responsible for our choices, and we will have to answer for them. Learn to take a deep breath and think before reacting. There will be enough to apologize for while moving through separation or divorce, without adding to the list.

AFFIRMATION: Today I will pause to take a few deep breaths before reacting to negative stimulus. I will choose my reaction wisely.

February 5

This is a day of stillness and peace. —A Course in Miracles

We owe ourselves a day of stillness and peace every so often. During a difficult transition there is so much going on around and within us, we need an occasional day to assimilate what is happening.

It's important to take time to rest, to be still, to go on some kind of retreat away from home. If that's not possible, take time for private reflection.

AFFIRMATION: Today I will decide on how I can nurture myself during this difficult transition, realizing that as I do that, I create peace around me.

February 6

In the middle of difficulty lies opportunity. —Albert Einstein

Almost always, difficulty provides opportunity for growth and expansion. We may understand for the first time what it's like for others to be in pain, so our ability to empathize grows. Maybe we are forced to reach out to others and admit we need help, which is never easy. New friends may be made as we are pressured out of our old ways. The need for more money may push us into a different, more satisfying career.

The difference between difficulty and opportunity lies in our ability to remain conscious and alert to a new life on the horizon. Let's move in that direction rather than hold on to what is already gone.

AFFIRMATION: Today I will remain alert to the opportunity that lies within difficulty and begin to see each day as a blessing.

February 7

Cultivating a warmhearted feeling for others automatically puts the mind at ease and helps remove whatever fears and insecurities we may have. —His Holiness the Dalai Lama

During divorce the marital relationship becomes adversarial, at least some of the time, and for some couples argument and bitterness become the norm. It's common to forget all our partner's positive attributes and dwell only on the negative. With this dynamic present, we must protect ourselves from the return volley and stay on guard. The battle escalates as shots are fired from both sides.

An antidote to escalation is remembering that your partner is not all bad and there are things to like about him or her. While this may not be easy at first, the long-term gain is worth the effort. First, there is less fear if there is some positive interaction; and if one partner de-escalates, the other may too. While this is not guaranteed, there is a far greater chance for peace if both partners stop slinging mud at each other. It only takes one person to change the dynamic.

AFFIRMATION: Today I will remember that by cultivating some warmhearted feelings for those I am in conflict with, I will feel better and have less fear.

February 8

Always do right. This will gratify some people, and astonish the rest. — Mark Twain

One of the difficulties with the process of divorce is that acting badly, and sometimes dishonestly, is considered normal. This engenders a lose-lose situation. When one person is acting badly, the other may think they have to act badly too. What is often not obvious in the early stages is that wrangling over material things ends up costing more to both parties than if the parties were generous in the first place. On the other hand, if both partners decide to act with integrity, everyone wins.

AFFIRMATION: Today I will monitor my thinking and choose to act with integrity as much as I can.

February 9

It is something to be able to paint a particular picture or carve a statue, and so to make a few objects beautiful; but it is far more glorious to carve and paint the very atmosphere and medium through which we look...to affect the quality of the day, that is the highest of arts. — Henry David Thoreau

Our attitudes create our world—the world we see. We have a unique view of the world, as does everyone else. When we concentrate on what is going right we see differently than if we notice only what's going wrong. The more we concentrate on what is good, the more we see good. The same is true for viewing the negatives. We can always build a case either way.

Our attitudes permeate our homes, influence our workplace and affect the people in our lives. Being aware of them, we take the reins in creating our environment.

AFFIRMATION: Today I will be aware of my attitudes and focus on the positive aspects of my life.

February 10

It is not fair to ask of others what you are not willing to do yourself. — Eleanor Roosevelt

If we expect tolerance, forgiveness, consideration, generosity, co-operation, helpfulness, kindness and love from those around us, we need to be willing to give them as well. One of the quickest ways to receive is to give what we want for ourselves to another person. What goes around comes around—not necessarily from that particular person, but from someone else.

If we are not receiving what we need, we must ask why not? We don't receive by demanding, we receive by giving.

AFFIRMATION: Today I will look for an opportunity to give to another person.

February 11

One of the most important ways to manifest integrity is to be loyal to those who are not present. In doing so, we build the trust of those who are present. —Stephen R. Covey

It is so tempting to speak badly of a person we are angry with. When our world is upside down and we are afraid, it's natural to lash out at the person we perceive to be the cause. No good comes from this and much damage may result. We may think we are acting to save ourselves or to influence our children or friends, but in the long run negative actions produce negative outcomes.

To be known as a person with integrity is priceless. We are trusted and respected and given the benefit of the doubt where there otherwise may have been a question. It's worth the temporary cost of self-control. Damage control is a good thing.

AFFIRMATION: Today I will watch what I say about those who are not present.

February 12

Wherever you go, there you are. —Jon Kabat Zinn

We don't divorce ourselves. Whatever our part was in the demise of our relationship, it goes with us.

It is crucial to pay close attention to our share of the relationship's problems or we will be destined to make the same mistakes again. Let's learn as much as we can about our own shortcomings so we can avoid them in the future.

AFFIRMATION: Today I am willing to take responsibility and make necessary changes.

February 13

Every action generates a force of energy that returns to us in kind...what we sow is what we reap. And when we choose actions that bring happiness and success to others, the fruit of our karma is happiness and success. —Deepak Chopra

Understanding that our actions create reactions, and that all we give will eventually return, can help us act with trust and integrity. While the desire for revenge is not unusual after a separation, seeking revenge makes things worse—for ourselves and for others. Revenge exacts a price from everyone.

In contrast, when we choose to take the high road we are rewarded by peace of mind, and hostility de-escalates. Our children are major beneficiaries of our mature choices.

AFFIRMATION: Today I will pause before reacting to consider the long-term results of my actions.

February 14

Let us be grateful for all the different kinds of love we have in our lives.

Let's celebrate love today. As we know, there are many kinds of love other than romantic love. There's the love of our children, parents, friends, family and our pets. There's the love our Higher Power has for us that is always there, whether or not we are aware of it. There may be a close connection with a co-worker to celebrate.

If we have none of these connections, we can give love to someone by making a phone call to cheer a person, visiting someone who is ill or sitting with an elderly person who might enjoy some company. Giving love is as good as receiving it. Sometimes it's even better.

AFFIRMATION: Today I will think about all the people whom I love and who love me. If I don't have enough of them, I'll be sure I have more by this time next year.

February 15

Be not afraid of life. Believe that life is worth living and your belief will help create the fact. —William James

Whether we are in a relationship or not, the quality of our lives is up to us. Becoming single again requires a big adjustment but once the adjustment is made and the change has taken place, life can become worth living again. To the surprise of many of us, life is better than ever.

In contrast, believing our life is over, that nothing good will happen again, fosters decisions and actions that close doors and create fear. Let's not make that mistake.

Major life-shifts offer opportunities for reinvention. Our belief that life is worth living will invite us to make decisions that create a new full life. Regardless of our circumstances, the choice of how we think is up to us.

AFFIRMATION: Today I will not allow myself to become immersed in negativity, and I will hold on to at least one positive thought all day.

February 16

Never underestimate a gesture of affection. —Unknown

Warmth and affection are very important for our health and well-being, especially during separation and divorce. Hugs are good medicine when given by safe people and benefit both giver and receiver.

Some of us have been deprived of touch for a long time. We may think this longing can only be gratified by romance and sex. The truth is that friendly hugs can go a long way in making us feel connected and cared for.

AFFIRMATION: Today I will ask for a hug from someone I trust and feel the warmth that it brings to my being.

February 17

An unexamined life is not worth living. —Socrates

Life presents us with many choices. One of the most important is to decide whether we will proactively engage in designing our future or accept what is given to us.

One of life's best teachers is the past. We can examine what we did and didn't like, the type of people we have loved, the kind of work we've done, how we have raised children, and whether we're satisfied with the decisions we've made. Only we can answer these questions for ourselves. If we don't do this exploration, we will have to be happy with what comes our way. In most cases, that is not enough.

AFFIRMATION: Today I will think about what makes me happy— and what doesn't.

February 18

It is better to light one candle than curse the darkness.
  —Motto of the Christopher Society

Are we victims? Maybe. Do we feel alone at times? Yes. Are we afraid of the dark? Sometimes. Can we become overwhelmed by the negativity of the situation? Yes. Are we powerless over our own state? Definitely not.

Lighting one candle may be reaching out to someone who feels worse than we do. It may be calling a friend or hugging a child. Making one small positive gesture can create many positive ripples. It's worth a try and better than encouraging darkness.

AFFIRMATION: Today I will be a light for myself and perhaps for someone else.

February 19

It's okay to look back, but don't stare. —Unknown

It's important that we understand how we came to our present circumstances. This is always true. In separation and divorce, however, it is possible to spend too much time in the past reliving what happened before.

Usually this stems from fear of the unknown. We look back so we don't have to look toward the future because we are afraid of what we may or may not imagine there. Staring at the past stops us from creating the future in a healthy and constructive way.

Looking back leaves us sad and stuck. Being proactive about our future is what makes life fun and interesting when we get there.

AFFIRMATION: Today I will think about what will make me happy a year from now and work toward that goal a little every day.

February 20

The greatest thing in this world is not so much where we are,
but in which direction we are moving. —Oliver Wendell Holmes

The end of a relationship creates a crossroads, a turning point, a fork in the road. We do not stay here—even if we want to, which most of us don't. There are any number of directions we can take. What's the best direction for our highest good?

AFFIRMATION: Today I will create a mental picture of what I want and see myself walking toward it.

February 21

I've learned that if you pursue happiness, it will elude you. But if you focus on your family, the needs of others, your work, meeting new people, and doing the very best you can, happiness will find you. —Andy Rooney

By following these suggestions, achieving happiness is within our domain. We don't have to wait for someone to love us, or to be married or in a relationship to be happy. Material wealth doesn't make us happy in the long run either. It's not enough.

When we engage in activities related to our family, the needs of others and our work, we will have returns. In contrast, when we become self-absorbed, thinking only about how miserable and lonely we are, we aren't doing anything to move toward happiness.

In doing the best we can, we avoid future guilt and regret. Even if we don't achieve the desired result, we know we tried our best and that will give us peace of mind.

AFFIRMATION: Today I won't allow myself to think that I can't be happy until someone else does what I think they should do. Instead, I'll be proactive about expanding my own happiness.

February 22

Nurture your mind with great thoughts, for you will never go higher than you think. —Benjamin Disraeli

I realized at the time of my divorce that I didn't know enough about healthy relationships, or how to help my children go through my divorce, or what I wanted in my new life. I knew what I didn't want but I needed guidance about what might be good for me.

If you admire the way someone handled her breakup or his divorce, ask how they did it. Ask people you respect for book recommendations and for other sources of good information. There is also a reading list at the back of this book.

AFFIRMATION: Today I will seek information so that I may create the best new life possible.

February 23

Never look down on anybody unless you're helping him up.
   —The Reverend Jesse Jackson

A hallmark of a breakup is judgment. We judge ourselves, our partners, our families and friends to make a case for what and who is right and who's on which side. Making all these judgments is exhausting and destroys our peace of mind.

It's not important whether we are better or worse than another person. Time can be spent more productively by making improvements in ourselves and reaching out to others. This is what brings serenity.

AFFIRMATION: Today when I find myself being judgmental, I will let go and seek serenity by helping instead of judging.

February 24

I will be open to discovering more talents and gifts within me. I will no longer put off that one thing that I have been afraid to try.
   —Unknown

A gift of the separation process is that we are cracked wide open and have an opportunity to see much more of ourselves than we ever have. Generally we use only a portion of our abilities based on what is needed at the time. In separation and divorce we are forced to review our past and think about the future. Believe it or not, *this is good.*

Where we may get into trouble is when we only want to review and hold on to the past. While this is normal for a while, if we become mired there we miss an extraordinary opportunity to be creative with our own lives. As we look at the many ways we have transformed and met challenges, what talents and abilities can we identify? We can make a list and be bold about it. We are responsible for creating our future, so we want to be aware of the many talents that already exist within us.

AFFIRMATION: Today I will take a step toward discovering more of my talents and abilities, knowing that there are many to be found.

February 25

I am aware of my limits and I honor them.
I give myself permission to keep my life simple.
I create the time to do things which nourish me.
　—Sue Patton Thoele

Breakups create temporary chaos, upheaval and exhaustion. For a while we do not operate at our normal level of ability. It's like trying to work with the flu—we are in pain, our heads are fuzzy, and all we want to do is sleep. This is a normal and temporary condition but it does create limits for us. For our well-being it's important to be understanding and cut ourselves some slack.

On days when we feel like this, we should feed ourselves foods that keep our bodies healthy and energized. Junk food, while easy and temporarily satisfying, makes us feel worse in the long run.

It's also important to get enough rest. If sleep won't come, lie down and rest, listen to some soothing music, and perhaps read some uplifting material. Identify other little things you can do to care for yourself. What makes you feel good or refreshed? A walk? A talk? A bath?

AFFIRMATION: Today I will think about what nourishes me, and I will have it available so I can take good care of myself.

February 26

The biggest mistake you can make is to believe you work for someone else.
—Unknown

The ultimate goal of our jobs is to provide the material structure for our lives. Whether we work for a corporation, in our own business or are raising a family, the way in which we do our work has a significant impact in other areas of our lives.

This may be a time when re-evaluation of our work is necessary. Some of us have to work smarter to make more money, some not as hard so we can spend time with our children. In either case, we need to keep in mind that we are working for ourselves. It's our job to evaluate whether our current work situation fills our needs.

AFFIRMATION: Today I will think about how I might improve my situation at work.

February 27

It doesn't interest me to know where you live or how much money you have. I want to know if you can get up after the night of grief and despair, weary and bruised to the bone, and do what needs to be done for the children.

—Oriah Mountain Dreamer, Indian Elder

This quotation from a inspirational book, titled *The Invitation*, speaks of character. When a significant relationship falls apart, pain and fear are very intense. However, the children still need us. They did not create this situation and still rely on us to do our job as parents—and they have a right to ask that of us.

Most parents have the character to put their pain aside and do what needs to be done. This sacrifice will pay many dividends in the future because the attention we give our kids now, enhances their well-being and ensures their healthy growth and development.

AFFIRMATION: Today I will take some time to be with my children.

February 28

When you get to be older and the concerns of the day have all been attended to and you turn to the inner life...well, if you don't know where it is, you'll be sorry. —Joseph Campbell

If you don't already have an inner life, this is a good time to develop one. Cultivating spirituality—the inner life—is important for balance. Having a connection with our Higher Power relieves loneliness and fear and creates a feeling of inner peace.

This may be accomplished in as many ways as there are people, since spirituality is intensely personal. At the back of this book is a list of books to further your exploration. Journaling and meditation are other ways to connect, as are going to church or temple. It's never too late to connect with a Higher Power, whatever our definition.

AFFIRMATION: Today I will think about how much an inner life may mean to me when I am older, and choose an avenue of spiritual practice that I am comfortable with.

March 1

An exercise to practice loving ourselves:

*For the next month say over and over to yourself "I approve of myself."
Do this three or four hundred times a day. No, it's not too many times.
When you are worrying, you go over your problem at least that many
times. Let "I approve of myself" become a walking mantra, something
you just say over and over to yourself almost nonstop. When negative
thoughts come up in response to this, give them no importance. Gently
say this to the thought, "I let you go, I approve of myself." If you can get
through your resistance, the results will be phenomenal.* —Louise Hay

When our self-esteem is going downhill, everything else seems to
go downhill with it. It's important to break this momentum and
change our negative self-talk quickly. This exercise is one way to
do that.

AFFIRMATION: Today I will do this exercise, even if it seems unfamiliar, and monitor how it makes me feel.

March 2

*What a gift of grace to be able to take the chaos from within and from it
create some semblance of order.* —Katherine Paterson

What seems to be never-ending chaos eventually does fall into
some semblance of order when we decide to create peace in our
lives. Some of us become addicted to chaos, particularly those
who experienced a lot of it growing up. Chaos may become the
normal state of affairs. Those of us who grew up with it continue
to create it because it feels familiar and we may not know how to
create anything else.

Many of us know people who have been divorced for many
years and still can't let the anger and bitterness go. They re-create
the chaos of a failed marriage and bitter divorce because they
don't know how to create something new. There are many ways
to learn how to create a wonderful life, regardless of the present
chaos.

AFFIRMATION: Today I'll ask my Higher Power to help me let go of the chaos and think about how I can build peace and order into my life.

March 3

Out of clutter, find simplicity. —Albert Einstein

Much emphasis is placed on keeping things when we go through divorce. We fight to hold on to items because of the "principle." I may not want it but *you* can't have it, so I'll fight for it.

Possessions tie us down to the status quo. The more we have, the more we want to protect it. The more time we spend protecting stuff, the less we have for relationships, fun and self-development. The more stuff we have, the less freedom, so this may be a time to actually enjoy unloading.

AFFIRMATION: Today I will think about what it may cost to hold on to more than I actually need.

March 4

The willingness to accept responsibility for one's own life is the source from which self-respect springs. —Joan Didion

Our lives today are the result of the choices we have made. While it may be difficult to see the past in this light, if we don't accept this, our future is bound to be the same as our past.

Once we decide that we are not victims and in fact have lots of creative power in our lives, we can begin to shape a life that is wonderful and meaningful. We don't have to accept someone else's view of what is right for us; we have the reins when we're ready to take them.

AFFIRMATION: Today I will stop blaming others for my state and think about my personal power to change what I can about myself.

March 5

The trick is to respect yourself and the other person at the same time. —
Stephen C. Paul

If you are expecting your former partner to continue to support
your children or yourself—or to take primary responsibility for
raising your children—wouldn't you want to have that person in
as good condition as possible? Isn't their physical and mental
health important for the good of the whole? What are the ramifications of distressing our partners by denying their legitimate
needs or seeking revenge?

When we are angry, and we often are in divorce, we may be
tempted to hurt our former partner. It is indeed a challenge to respect ourselves and the other person at the same time, but doing
so may pay big dividends later on. If we can't muster respect, we
can choose not to do damage.

AFFIRMATION: Today I will consider the big picture before I react
in a negative way.

March 6

Listen.

Clear communication is always challenging. During a breakup it
may seem impossible because we are vulnerable and sensitive to
much of what our partner says. It's easy to misunderstand and
react inappropriately because of the strong emotions present.

During a conversation that is highly charged, it's important to
listen carefully and clarify what we don't understand before reacting. In this way we make sure we are not reacting negatively
to something we perceived, but wasn't actually said.

AFFIRMATION: Today, when fear starts to rise during a conversation, I will take a few deep breaths and listen attentively to what
is being said to be sure I understand the other person's point of
view before responding.

March 7

We must use time as a tool, not as a couch. —John F. Kennedy

Time flies, whether we are having fun or not. Divorce creates tremendous challenge in all areas of our lives. To create the best life possible for ourselves we need to be proactive and not assume our needs will be met.

There is a recovery period that requires rest and self-care but we must not get stuck there. Do we need more friends, more education, less aggravation or some therapy? A great new life requires action!

AFFIRMATION: Today I will think about what actions I can take to create a great new life.

March 8

Change is not made without inconvenience, even from worse to better. —Unknown

There are many, many changes that occur during separation. Actually there are always changes occurring in our lives, but in divorce the number seems to double or triple.

Just because change may be difficult doesn't mean it shouldn't happen or that we don't recover from it. When we look back at our lives in a year or two, we may see that the forced change has created a pivotal time of growth for us and one we would not have wanted to miss.

AFFIRMATION: Today I will look at change as a transition to a new and better place, rather than something to be avoided.

March 9

Our job is not merely to discover ourselves, but to create new selves in the new context.

We have so much potential! Most of us use much less of our creative ability than we have, getting into a routine and staying there for long periods of time. After all, there is only so much we can do in a day.

While separation is a painful process, the upside is that we can decide again who we want to be. As the pieces of our lives are tossed in the air, we can put them together in a different way as they come down and add some new pieces to the picture too.

What separates the drones from the artists is the ability to arrange the pieces in a way that engenders happiness and improves the picture. If we don't know how to do that, we need to seek some help—see a financial advisor, a therapist, or a travel agent, join a group, read some literature, take a class—however we decide to do it, the point is to become *proactive*.

AFFIRMATION: Today, rather than looking back, I will think about who I want to be in the next phase of my life and the steps needed to get me there.

March 10

Every action taken by human beings is based in love or fear...Fear is the energy which contracts, closes down, draws in, runs, hides, hoards, harms. Love is the energy which expands, opens up, sends out, stays, reveals, shares, heals. Every human thought, word or deed is based in one emotion or the other. You have no choice about this, because there is nothing else from which to choose. But you have free choice about which of these to select. —Neale Donald Walsch

It's easy to feel during separation or divorce that there is no love in our lives and that we have much to fear. That's because many of us tend to perceive love as coming from one person, and when we no longer have that person, there is no love for us. When we are not in a loving state, fear creeps in.

Love is our birthright. It comes from our Higher Power and flows like energy through the universe. Being *in love* means something different. We can experience love in many ways and yet not be *in love* with a particular person. Loving energy, as the quotation describes, feels wonderful. Fearful energy shuts us down. We have the choice, under any circumstance, to choose our state.

AFFIRMATION: Today I will monitor my emotional state to determine whether I am experiencing love or fear. If I am in fear, I will ask my Higher Power to help me get back to love.

March 11

Bloom where you're planted. —Unknown

Why wait to bloom? If we need the perfect circumstances to be happy, we will wait a good long time. Learning to bloom wherever we are is an art worth cultivating because we will create a good life even in difficult circumstances.

If we are unhappy at work, instead of doing a mediocre job, we need to do the best possible job. This is the way to a better position. If we are at home raising children, we can be the best possible parent we can be. If we are doing both, we do the best we can, understanding that the demands of a dual career are taxing. We do the best we can wherever we are, and that will lead us to a better place.

What a marvelous example we can be for our children. They will learn to pursue excellence. This does not mean having to be perfect, but to make the most of our present circumstances.

AFFIRMATION: Today I will do the best job I can and know that I will reap the benefits later.

March 12

Character is what you are in the dark. —Dwight Lyman Moody

What it all boils down to is that we have to sleep at night. We have to live with ourselves. Character is sorely tested during divorce, and to stick with our principles and beliefs under duress isn't easy.

Divorce is a temporary process with lifelong ramifications. No one is perfect and mistakes will happen, but it's important to be true to ourselves and not allow this situation to change our values and character. In a year or two we will be glad we acted in a way we can be proud of.

AFFIRMATION: Today I will recognize that when I am tempted to stray from what I know is right, taking the high road is in my best interest.

March 13

There is beauty before me, there is beauty behind me
There is beauty above me, there is beauty below me
I walk in beauty... —Navajo prayer

Sometimes we get stuck in our own thinking and it's good to look up and realize that there is much good around us. We don't want to miss it.

Let's say this prayer many times today and watch our perspectives change as we become open to the idea of beauty in our surroundings. Let's chant it to ourselves and observe our reactions as we become aware of the many gifts that our Higher Power has placed in our path.

AFFIRMATION: Today, as I go through my day, I will look for the beauty that is present in my world and let what I find lift my spirits.

March 14

There is beauty in me. There is beauty in you. Let my eyes be open.

There is beauty in every living thing. The more we allow ourselves to see beauty, the more we will be shown. If we can allow ourselves to see beauty in everyone we deal with, we will be happier. Perception is a choice.

AFFIRMATION: Today, as I go through my day, I will feel my own beauty and look for beauty in others. If I have trouble with this, I will ask my Higher Power to show me the loveliness present in myself and others.

March 15

The past is history
The future is a mystery
Now is a gift
That's why we call it the present. —Unknown

It's much more compelling to think about the past or the future during a breakup than to think about the present. When we ignore the present, however, we ignore our lives. We think about how wonderful or awful our past was and how frightening and different the future seems but we may never look at the gifts today holds. Being able to enjoy the present is the key to enjoying life!

There are always positive and negative things going on around us, and in this very minute we choose the ones to think about. While we need to handle some difficult things, we can also be aware of the gifts that the present offers.

Creativity happens in the present moment. We can create change *now*, we can enjoy life *today*. We can't change something that has already happened, nor can we enjoy something that will happen later on. Today—now—is where the rest of our life begins.

AFFIRMATION: Today I will spend as much time as possible in the ever-present NOW.

March 16

No act of kindness, no matter how small, is ever wasted. —Aesop

When we perform an act of kindness the first beneficiary is ourselves. Being kind to another person makes us feel good and is its own reward.

When we perform a kind act for another, we alter the person's perspective for the moment, for the day and maybe forever. And there may be a ripple effect from a kind act that we will be unaware of but that can go on and on, touching many people. These are the things that rarely make the news but happen among human beings all the time.

AFFIRMATION: Today I will look for opportunities to be kind so I can experience the joy of giving.

March 17

May the road rise to meet you,
May the wind be always at your back,
May the sun shine warm upon your face,
May the rain fall soft upon your fields,
And until we meet again,
May God hold you in the palm of his hand. —*an Irish blessing*

How lovely it feels to wish others well from the heart—to bless them and appreciate them. We may or may not be feeling wonderful, but rising to the occasion of wishing another person well will cause our spirits to rise along with theirs.

Hearing something warm and appreciative can make a person's day. All of us can use more love and blessings in our lives.

AFFIRMATION: Today I will be a distributor of cheer and good wishes.

March 18

Value yourself. The only people who appreciate a doormat are people with dirty shoes. —Leo Buscaglia

We will not be valued until we value ourselves. Some of us were trained as children to serve others, or maybe we were trained to just stay out of the way. Whatever our past was, we can work in the present to change the future. If we have a hard time valuing ourselves, we can go into therapy for a while to learn how to do it.

To avoid being hurt again, we may choose another partner who is needier than we are. We may feel safe, assuming they need us more than we need them. This is an illusion.

Another way to value ourselves is to find the healthiest person we can, but in order to attract a healthy person, we must be healthy ourselves.

Growth in this area will impact all future relationships in a positive way.

AFFIRMATION: Today I will value myself by making a list of all of my positive attributes and read them three times a day for the next week.

March 19

Where you stand depends on where you sit. —Miles Law

This statement is important to keep in mind when negotiating. In other words, we all have our points of view—and from our own perspective, ours are valid and justifiable. We need to understand where the other person is coming from and take that perspective seriously. We needn't agree, but we need to understand.

AFFIRMATION: Today I will think about where I stand on key issues and be ready to communicate my position clearly.

March 20

Every soul has its own path to follow.

Everyone, whether in a relationship or not, has a life to lead and a path to follow. The path is different for everyone. Sometimes we are meant to walk the same path with another for a time and then we come to a fork where each person has to choose a direction. If their life requires a different path than our own, we must let them go their way and we must go on with ours.

When we overcome our anger and hurt that our partner chose a different road, we may be able to maintain a relationship, but the relationship will require a new configuration. If we have children in common, for example, we must move from an intimate to a business relationship. This can be done in time and with a mature vision for the future.

AFFIRMATION: Today I will let go and allow others to be who and where they are.

March 21

All attack is a call for help. —A Course in Miracles

Because there are only two states, love and fear, when we attack another person fear is always behind it. It may not be immediately obvious where the fear is coming from, but you can believe that it's in there somewhere. We may be afraid of being hurt, abandoned, having no money or a place to live or, worse yet, of feeling unloved. We fight to protect what we have or want. We don't want anything taken away.

The irony of attack is it brings us to the opposite of what we want. We attract love by being loving, abundance by being generous, kindness and consideration by being kind and considerate. When we attack, we get retaliation, which then escalates, bringing more hurt and feelings of abandonment.

AFFIRMATION: Today I will think about attack as a call for help and try not to respond in kind. (This is difficult, but it's an advanced lesson.)

March 22

I live in the present.
I can courageously handle anything as long as I take it one moment at a time.
This too shall pass. —Sue Patton Theole

One way to get through divorce without going insane is to realize that in time, the process will end and our life will go on. Instead of dwelling on all the horrible things that *might* happen, we must focus on one task at a time. When anxiety rises, we can choose one point of attention and stick with it.

Doing even one small task a day toward a goal builds self-esteem and self-confidence and creates momentum.

AFFIRMATION: Today I will choose one task that will bring me closer to my goal and accomplish it. Then I will congratulate myself for doing what needed to be done.

March 23

Love doesn't die but sometimes it's invisible.

Divorce is so painful because it is adversarial and because there's not supposed to be any love in it. That's why we divorce. Because there's no love, right? This is generally not true.

No matter how painful the marriage has become and how happy we may be to be out of it, if there was love to begin with, it's still there. Most likely something changed over time that made it difficult to live together. This doesn't mean we have to hate each other, only that we have to accept the change and adjust our lives accordingly. Change might be good, even if we didn't want it in the beginning.

Sometimes it lessens the pain to acknowledge that love does exist, while realizing that circumstances have changed. We can still have love for that person while moving on, meeting others and creating a new life. Hatred is not mandatory and is actually quite debilitating.

AFFIRMATION: Today I will keep in mind that loving is better for me than hating and that there is more than one kind of love to feel. I may not love the other as a spouse, but I can love him or her as a person.

March 24

When we truly care for ourselves, it becomes possible to care profoundly about other people. The more alert and sensitive we are to our own needs, the more loving and generous we can be toward others. —Eda LeShan

Sometimes being alone creates our first opportunity in many years to take a look at what *we* really need. This task helps us realize who we are and what we expect from our lives today. It's like taking a snapshot of the present.

Now we have an opportunity for self-examination and self-nurturance. If we take care of ourselves, we will be in condition to nurture our children. We may think that taking care of ourselves is selfish, but in fact it gives us the strength to care for others.

AFFIRMATION: Today and every day I will take care of myself. I will rest when I'm tired, eat when I'm hungry, call a friend when I'm lonely. I will see a doctor, dentist or therapist when necessary. I will upgrade and maintain my appearance because that makes me feel good.

March 25

Explore your higher latitudes...be a Columbus to whole new continents and worlds within you, open new channels, not of trade but of thought.
—Henry David Thoreau

We all are capable of much more than we think. We mustn't limit ourselves by what we were able or unable to do before. Divorce is a gateway to our potential and forces us to explore our abilities. If we don't know how to do something, we should find out from someone who does. There are experts available and books that teach what we need to know.

If we spend time taking care of our own business and maximizing our abilities, rather than wishing things were different, the positive gains and growth will be amazing. We don't have to make great strides all at once, just a little each day.

AFFIRMATION: Today I will be open to developing abilities and character traits that will enhance my future. I will not allow my thinking to be defined by my old limitations.

March 26

Do not fear death so much, but rather the inadequate life.
—Bertolt Brecht

No one wants to grow old alone. That thought seems unbearable, yet it will happen to many of us. Marriage or having a partner doesn't protect us from being alone at the end because we may not be the one who dies first.

Choosing to make our lives rich and wonderful is our protection against the inadequate life, and that choice must be made now. Fostering loving relationships with our children, siblings and friends, enjoying a creative outlet and having passionate interests are what make life worth living. We can always choose to share our lives with a partner again but if our lives are already full, we will choose a mate from a state of completeness, not neediness.

AFFIRMATION: Today I will enrich my life. This is my privilege and responsibility.

March 27

Find new ways to keep your spirits up until that telephone rings, t.
ter arrives, that new opportunity comes knocking at your door. I
smile on your face, listen to oldies on the radio, look at old photos. Dis\..act
yourself with a positive project—rearrange the furniture in a room. Get
outside, window shop, walk the dog, buy an ice cream cone, fly a kite, play
games with a child, take a ride in the country. —Arthur Pine

In other words, if we want to feel better we have to do something
different to change the mood. If we learn to take care of ourselves
in this way, we will gain personal power. We will be able to manage our emotional state by ourselves and not expect another to do
it for us. This is a skill that's important now and in future relationships.

There is no benefit to being depressed. It's a natural state during
a breakup but we don't have to cultivate it.

AFFIRMATION: Today, if I feel sad, I will do something that will
make me feel better. If I don't know what makes me feel better, I'll
try some new things and experiment. My mood is in my control.

March 28

Let me not pray to be sheltered from dangers,
    but to be fearless in facing them.
Let me not beg for the stilling of my pain
    but for the heart to conquer it.
Let me not look for allies in life's battlefield
    but to my own strength.
Let me not crave in anxious fear to be saved
    but hope for the patience to win my freedom.
Grant me that I may not be a coward,
    feeling your mercy in my success alone;
    but let me find the grasp of Your hand in my failure.
    —Rabindranath Tagore

This prayer is about self-reliance and growth. When we know
that we can withstand what life hands us and go beyond our
former limitations with each experience, we begin to feel confident and strong.

To be a victim is to stay in a place of powerlessness. Let's choose strength for ourselves.

AFFIRMATION: Today, if I'm overcome by fear, I will pray that the pain I experienced will be transformed into growth.

March 29

There is a first and a second creation to every part of your life. You are either the first creation of your proactive design, or you are the second creation of circumstances, past habits, or other people's agendas. — Stephen R. Covey

Take yourself seriously. What do you want? What do you need? Will you rely on others to give it to you, or will you get what you need regardless of what others do?

We are powerful. We may need help in certain areas and there's nothing wrong with that. But there's a lot we can do for ourselves and by doing that we get stronger and stronger.

AFFIRMATION: Today I will be creative with my life and not let old habits stand in the way of my development.

March 30

Learning is finding out what you already know.
Doing is demonstrating that you know it.
Teaching is reminding others that they know
*   just as well as you.*
You are all learners, doers, teachers. —Richard Bach

The wonderful thing about belonging to a support group while going through divorce and separation is that we learn and teach all the time. What one doesn't know, another does. Information is exchanged and shared—saving time, frustration and aggravation.

  When we take action based on what we've learned, we become an example for others.

AFFIRMATION: Today I will be all three: learner, teacher and doer.

March 31

We turn not older with years, but newer every day.
  —Emily Dickinson

We have an opportunity to expand and transform every day. We limit the depth of our relationships when we believe we know all there is to know about another person. This is never true, regardless of how close we are because we are exposed to new people and incorporate new ideas all the time.

  An idea in a book or a movie may have a profound effect on our thinking or we may have a conversation with someone whose attitude, job or adventure expands our horizons. Daily incidents change us in large or small ways but we are always becoming new.

AFFIRMATION: Today I will learn something new about one person who is close to me.

April 1

Work and live to serve others, to leave the world a little better than you found it and garner for yourself as much peace of mind as you can. This is happiness. —David Sarnoff

A lot of us think that happiness comes from being given something. This places us in a passive position, only being happy when something comes our way. We may try to manipulate a person or situation to further our happiness. We may justify our position and not care if it's in the other person's best interest. This doesn't bring happiness.

Happiness comes from giving. Love comes from loving. Giving and loving are actions we can take and the source of true joy. What goes around comes around. Happiness and love are by-products of our actions, so we get a return—but maybe not in the way we expect it.

AFFIRMATION: Today I will perform an anonymous act of kindness and notice how that makes me feel.

April 2

If we did all the things we are capable of doing, we would literally astound ourselves. —Thomas Alva Edison

It is well known that human beings use only a small percentage of their brain. Divorce is a time when we must stretch into new areas. Isn't it good to know that we have so much untapped potential?

AFFIRMATION: Today I will make a list of all the things I would like to do, then pick one and determine what I already know about it. Then I will go about learning more—even if it's only a little at a time. When I've accomplished the first ability, I'll go on to the next.

April 3

Collect adventures and experiences, not things. Things will burden you. Adventures and experiences will give you pleasant memories. — William D. Montpart

It's hard to realize when one is in the middle of a fight over property that any one thing is not that important. The item may be valuable and still not important. It helps to realize that our peace of mind is more important than any one item. Getting rid of stuff is actually very liberating. We feel lighter and cleaner and ready to begin a new chapter of life.

Adventures, experiences and education are the important aspects of life. Relationships and what we have done, learned and experienced will keep us company when we're older. They add to who we are as a person and make us interesting and fun to be around.

AFFIRMATION: Today I will plan an adventure for myself.

April 4

There are no times in life when opportunity, the chance to be and do, gathers so richly about the soul as when it has to suffer. Then everything depends on whether the man turns to the lower or the higher helps. If he resorts to mere expedients and tricks, the opportunity is lost. He comes out no richer nor greater; nay, he comes out harder, poorer, smaller, for his pain. But if he turns to God, the hour of suffering is the turning hour of his life.
—Phillips Brooks

I turned to God because I was desperate, afraid and had nowhere else to turn. I had been attending Al-Anon meetings because of an alcohol problem in the family, and had heard about turning my life over to God but I couldn't seem to do it.

When my husband and I separated, our four children were adolescents, which meant I had to parent them by myself most of the time. We lived in a house that I couldn't afford to keep on my own. I had many worries and decisions that I was ill-equipped to make. I often woke up at night in a panic, thinking "What if..."

It was then, with my back against the wall, that I made the decision to turn to God for help, and my life has steadily improved ever since.

AFFIRMATION: Today I will do the best I can, and even if I don't trust the result, I will ask God for help with one problem and watch for an answer.

Note: Some of us pray for help, get it, and then assume it's coincidence or something other than God's help. Make sure to recognize prayer's effectiveness and to say thank You.

April 5

The Serenity Prayer
God, grant me the serenity
to accept the things I cannot change,
the courage to change the things I can
and the wisdom to know the difference. —Reinhold Niebuhr

Twelve Step groups of all kinds use the Serenity Prayer to invoke a Higher Power to help sort out the issues that cause pain and stress. Those of us who live with the problems of divorce can easily relate to the things we can and cannot change or control, as well as to the need for serenity.

From this realization growth begins, because with time and practice we learn to spend our energy only on circumstances that are within our power to change. We become less overwhelmed, depressed, anxious and frustrated. The reward is feeling more composed, creative, peaceful and in charge of our lives.

AFFIRMATION: Today I will say the Serenity Prayer whenever I feel stress and notice the change in my state. (Note: Saying the prayer always helps but at times of particularly high stress, it helps to say it over and over, focusing on the meaning of each word, until we feel the shift.)

April 6

"Be comforted and walk your life in light and trust for nothing will come to that is not meant to be. There is nothing that can happen in your life that in any way threatens your soul. Indeed, all of life experience enhances its awareness. There is nothing that does not serve the process of your soul's growth."
—Pat Rodegast and Judith Stanton

It's comforting to know that we are on our own path. This doesn't depend on whether or not we are in a relationship. Sometimes, in fact, a relationship hides or blocks our path. We get so caught up and involved with another we may forget we have our own development and growth to attend to.

Try experiencing divorce as a path being cleared. We are invited to get back on track or begin a new journey.

AFFIRMATION: Today I will think about what I am meant to do with my life from today forward.

April 7

I pause and absorb what people say before I respond.
I have the courage to ask others to hear me.
My goal is to understand and have my words reflect what's in my heart.
—Sue Patton Thoele

When emotions run high, it's easy to misunderstand another out of defensiveness. One of the biggest challenges in divorce is really hearing what the other person is saying. Most of us feel a blow more often than was intended. If we have the ability to attentively listen until the other person is finished, we have the right to ask that we be listened to in the same way. If we can do this, we'll save a lot of attorney's fees.

The more we speak from a knowledge of what we really want and the more deeply we understand the other, the easier the process becomes for everyone. For example, don't let an attorney speak for you in a way that doesn't reflect your true feelings and thinking.

AFFIRMATION: Today I will make a decision not to fund my attorney's next trip to Hawaii, by listening and taking a few deep breaths before responding. If I need more time before I respond, I will ask for it.

April 8

The beautiful souls are they that are universal, open, and ready for all things. —Michel Eyquem de Montaigne

Some of us were raised in a home with a lot of fear. Our parents may have sternly cautioned that we would become severely ill if we went out with a wet head, didn't have sweater on, or sat in a draft or on pavement. It may have gone on and on. Some parents attempt to protect their children to such a degree that even as middle-aged adults, we have to tell ourselves that we'll be okay when we try something new.

Judgment—of others, of experiences, of what's safe—shuts us down. Notice that those who judge and talk badly of others are not happy. The less we judge the more universal and open we become.

AFFIRMATION: Today I will be aware of my judgments and suspend them as much as possible, then observe how that changes my state of mind.

April 9

...Know that what you do in the time of your greatest trial can be your greatest triumph. For the experience you create is a statement of Who You Are—and Who You Want To Be.
   —Neale Donald Walsch

Who do we want to be? Divorce is an open door and a time for great transformation. Whether we want it or not, change will occur, so we may as well create ourselves in the best possible way.

If we can do our best in times of great trial, self-esteem will grow proportionately. Let's turn this challenge into a triumph.

AFFIRMATION: Today I will act according to my vision of who I want to be.

April 10

If rejection destroys your self-esteem, you're letting others hold you as an emotional hostage. —Stephen R. Covey

Rejection is a tough issue for most of us. It is hard for everyone, but the closer and more trusted a person is, the harder it is to defend our self-esteem from rejection. Most of us need temporary help with this.

Therapy, support groups and daily readings are tools for increasing self-esteem. Why not get as much help as we can as we go through such a difficult period? This is not the time to do it alone.

AFFIRMATION: Today I'll do what I can to increase my self-esteem and not leave that to someone else.

April 11

Let us be grateful to people who make us happy—they are the charming gardeners who make our souls bloom. —Marcel Proust

We may be putting a lot of demands on our friends to support us and listen to our woes; and because we are sad, we forget that they also have important things going on and problems to solve in their own lives.

Do something nice for a person who has been supportive: buy them a card, bake them some brownies, take them to lunch or call just to thank them for their friendship. (Leave it at that—don't use the call as an excuse to get back into your own agenda.)

AFFIRMATION: Today, to make myself feel good, I will make a list of those who have been there for me and decide how to do something nice for each one of them.

April 12

I awoke this morning with devout thanksgiving for my friends, the old and the new. —Ralph Waldo Emerson

Don't go through divorce alone—make some new friends. Some of our old friends have an adjustment to make because they need to realign themselves with us in a new context. Some will make that adjustment and some won't.

Find a divorce support group and join it. If you can't find one, start one. We need to make new friends who understand what we're going through and aren't telling us that it's been six months and we should be over it by now. Even therapists may not understand how long it takes to work through the ending of a long-term relationship.

Let's be open to new people and new ideas. We may be grateful for our old friends, but we will benefit by expanding our horizons.

AFFIRMATION: Today I'll contact local resources such as houses of worship, social service agencies and pastoral counseling services to see if there are any support groups available.

April 13

The universe operates through dynamic exchange...giving and receiving are different aspects of the flow of energy in the universe. And in our willingness to give that which we seek, we keep the abundance of the universe circulating in our lives.
—Deepak Chopra

If we want love, we have to be loving. If we want forgiveness, we need to forgive. If we want people to say nice things about us, we have to say nice things about others. If we want to be treated fairly, we need to act fairly ourselves. If we don't want to be lied to, we need to tell the truth.

We cannot expect others to treat us better than we behave toward them. Let's keep abundance flowing in our lives by our willingness to give what we seek.

AFFIRMATION: Today I will give to others what I want to receive.

April 14

Pascal said, "All of humanity's problems stem from man's inability to sit quietly in a room alone." I'm not sure I would go quite this far, but I am certain that a quiet mind is the foundation of inner peace. And inner peace translates into outer peace.
—Richard Carlson, Ph.D.

Meditation is a wonderful thing. If you don't already do this, try it. If you normally do it, keep it up. Prayer is asking for answers, while meditation is listening for them. If our mind is always racing, we can't hear the answers; they can't get past the busy signal.

Inner peace is priceless. If we are at peace, we are better parents, we do better work, are more creative, think more clearly, make decisions effectively. The opposite of peace is chaos, and we all know how that feels. Cultivate peace in your life.

AFFIRMATION: Today I will take some time to meditate. If I don't know how, I will learn.

April 15

I'm glad that I understand that while language is a gift, listening is a responsibility. —Nikki Giovanni

Listening fully is a skill that few of us have developed, yet it is so important. Instead of listening, most of us hear the first few words the other person is saying and start to formulate a response in our mind without hearing the rest of the statement. What's more, some of us even complete the sentence for the other person!

In any relationship—whether at peace or at war—listening is much more important than talking. It's the only way things get done and issues are resolved.

AFFIRMATION: Today, for one entire conversation, I will listen to the other person until he or she is completely finished talking before I speak.

April 16

Avoid judging, agreeing, or disagreeing during highly emotional discussions.

STOP. Breathe. Take a break, take a walk, tell the person you'll call them back, breathe. Many mistakes are made in the heat of the moment that we regret within the next 24 hours.

Get into the habit of saying "I need to think about that," if you're not sure of what to do next. We don't have to have all the answers at our fingertips, and sometimes taking just a short break before speaking can save us a lot of trouble.

We'll be taken seriously if we take a break, think and then respond within a reasonable period. This technique should not be used to postpone a decision indefinitely. This is one way of taking care of ourselves.

AFFIRMATION: Today and every day, if I'm feeling very emotional, I will not make important decisions until I calm down.

April 17

It takes great courage and personal strength to hold on to our center during times of great hurt. It takes wisdom to understand that our reactiveness only fans the flames of false drama. Love creates a mystical shield around us, protecting us from chaos. When we are in the midst of loss, or betrayal, or crisis of any kind, there is power in the words, "Be still and know I am." —Marianne Williamson

Anyone can be nice when things are going well. The difficulty lies in retaining what we believe when we are challenged. When we are attacked, it feels like we should attack back. This is not in our best interest.

False drama is distracting and enervating and is usually a reaction to something other than the issue at hand. When we ask our Higher Power to come into our center and be with us, we don't feel alone. Even if you don't believe spiritual comfort is possible, be open to the possibility.

AFFIRMATION: Today, when I'm feeling hurt, I will ask my Higher Power to be with me. I will suspend doubt and see how I feel.

April 18

Seize the day. —Horace

Life exists in the present. We can examine the past and either dread or look forward to the future, but if we are not looking at today, we aren't living our lives.

Life is happening NOW! Open your eyes. Be aware of what's around you. What do you see, smell, hear? What do you feel like doing right now? All too often we are connected to the past or are projected into the future and we don't look at the marvelous potential that today holds.

AFFIRMATION: Today when I'm tempted to plan far into the future or reminisce about the past, I will pull myself into the present moment, notice what today has to offer and take advantage of it.

April 19

Each friend represents a world in us, a world possibly not born until they arrive, and it is only by this meeting that a new world is born. — Anaïs Nin

Have you ever noticed that we are different with every person we know? We alter ourselves slightly in each relationship in order to mesh with another. Each person relates to us based on what we have in common. When we find a friend who has information and experience in an area of interest to us, we develop our interest that much further. A friend may open a new world to us when they introduce us to their family and friends, and we extend our world into theirs. Friends may also introduce us to something entirely new.

While it may be a temptation to isolate ourselves while we are going through divorce, we should stay in touch with friends. We need to expand our world.

AFFIRMATION: Today I will think about how grateful I am to have friends who care about me.

April 20

It's not what we say, or how we feel—it's what we do that defines us.

Talk the talk—anyone can do that. Walking the talk is what's important.

We teach or influence by example, and those who do not practice what they preach have no credibility.

AFFIRMATION: Today I'll make sure that what I do is consistent with what I say.

April 21

No man ever listened himself out of a job. —Calvin Coolidge

Concentration is more difficult under stressful circumstances. We find ourselves reviewing our situation and trying to find answers to problems all the time—whether we are at work or not.

It's important to take our jobs seriously, listen carefully to what is being asked of us and get clarification if necessary.

AFFIRMATION: Today I will listen carefully to what's being asked of me, to be sure that I fully understand.

April 22

We are all equal. Anyone who doesn't know that is miserable.
—Robert Kaufman

We are all equal, if not the same. Some of us may know more, have more money, be nicer, have a relationship with God, be great looking, be famous. But if we have to maintain a stance of being "better than...," we won't be able to look at any new information. At that point, we are probably out of touch with reality.

Competitiveness distracts us from what we are supposed to be doing—a good job. If we are concentrating on besting someone, we are not using our effort creatively because we have to keep one eye on the other person. We are each unique, having our own voice and outlook, and if we spend our time worrying about what someone else is doing, we will miss our own opportunities.

On the other hand, if we believe that we aren't as worthy as the next person we are mistaken as well. We are no better or worse than anyone else.

AFFIRMATION: Today I realize that I'm not inferior or superior to anyone else.

April 23

When a person does a good deed when he or she didn't have to, God looks down and smiles and says, "For this moment alone, it was worth creating the world." —The Talmud

We become our own worst enemy when we become self-consumed. Because of the pain we experience, it's not unusual to want to nurse our wounds, but nothing feels better than to do something nice for someone else. No matter how badly we feel, there is someone who could use a kind word or deed, more than we need to keep to ourselves.

What goes around comes around. No good deed goes unrewarded.

AFFIRMATION: Today I will reach out to someone who could use what I have to offer and notice how good that feels.

April 24

There is no duty we so much underrate as the duty of being happy. By being happy, we sow anonymous benefits upon the world. —Robert Louis Stevenson

It's okay to take time off from the stress. We can get so involved with pressing issues that we forget about the rest of life. Get out of the house, see a funny movie, go to the zoo, spend time with people you love. Get away from it for a while. Do it with the kids. Do it on your own. You'll come back with a fresh perspective. We don't get any points for suffering full-time.

AFFIRMATION: Today I will either get out or make plans to get out soon. I will have a plan for at least one activity that I like for every weekend.

April 25

Life is the first gift, love is the second, and understanding the third. — Marge Piercy

Understanding that love is all around me and that romantic love is not the only kind of love helped me feel better. When I was feeling like nobody loved me, I thought of my children. Then I thought of my friends. Then my dog. I began to feel better.

Then I realized again that to receive love I had to give it. If I hugged a friend, he or she would hug me back. If I took time to visit an elderly person, he or she would appreciate the company. If I took the time to call someone who needed cheering up, their response to my call would warm me. There's lots of love around but I may have to be the one willing to start its flow.

AFFIRMATION: Today I will look for opportunities to reach out and connect with others.

April 26

Decide who you are in relationship to the separation. Will it be a burial or a resurrection?

Some people fold after a separation or divorce. They never get over it, thinking about it as if it happened yesterday instead of years ago. They hold on to the hurt, become bitter and make this their connection to life.

There are others who, even though their existence has been dramatically altered, make a decision to create a new and satisfying life for themselves. They acknowledge their losses and feel the pain but choose to use their energy to create the best life they can. They understand that life is like a blank canvas and *we* choose the colors of the paint. We can paint a picture using black and gray or we can use any of the other colors, alone or in combination. No one can paint on our canvas but us.

AFFIRMATION: Today I will draw a picture of how I'd like my new life to be.

April 27

You can't change the world—you can only change yourself.

Although we can only change ourselves, making a change creates a ripple effect, like throwing a stone into a pond. When we change our behavior, the effects of that change may reach farther than we anticipate. We don't always see the big picture and realize the impact we have on others.

Step One (see January 4) suggests that we can't control others and that if we try, our own lives become unmanageable. We can only change ourselves. That's where our true power lies, and by working for change within ourselves, we often affect others in a way we couldn't do otherwise.

AFFIRMATION: Today instead of wishing things were different, I will concentrate on strengthening and improving *myself*.

April 28

Diagnose before prescribing. —Franklin Covey

Isn't it easy to give advice? It's easy to relate another person's problem to something in our own past or present, and then make some suggestions.

When presented with a problem, let's get all the facts and take time to think. At that point, we might come up with a solution that is meaningful. Too often, we think we have an answer without really understanding the problem.

AFFIRMATION: Today I will take time to think before I give advice. I will also weigh the value of advice given to me.

April 29

How important is language in shaping our experience of life? It's absolutely fundamental. Quite simply, the words we attach to our experience become our experience. —Tony Robbins

This is an important concept to grasp, particularly during the divorce process. Because we feel angry, defensive and acutely sensitive, we hear statements made by our (ex)spouse *through our own emotional filter.* This filter can slant our interpretation of what's being said. Then if we talk about it from our perspective, our spin becomes our reality, when in fact, the original intention may have been different. We may create a negative interaction because we are angry or hurt, rather than because of what's actually being said or done.

When we talk about our former partner in negative terms, those terms may eventually seem real and we may lose perspective on the total person. When we dwell on the negative aspects of our lives, we become depressed.

So whenever possible, let's protect our mental health by looking for neutral or positive terms when describing our experience.

AFFIRMATION: Today I will become aware of how the words I choose to describe my experience create my emotional filter.

April 30

When we recall the past, we usually find that it is the simplest things — not the great occasions — that in retrospect give off the greatest glow of happiness. —Bob Hope

The simple things are the everyday happenings that we can easily overlook, like having breakfast with the kids, taking a walk with a friend, cooking a meal or noticing a sunset.

When we are living through a breakup we may feel that the glow of happiness is out of our reach, but all we have to do is stay alert to opportunities and celebrate them as they are found. Our quality of life is determined by whether or not we can enjoy the little details of daily life.

Another way to find happiness is to be happy for someone else. It's easy to feel resentment toward others whose lives are going well, but feeling that way deprives us of extra opportunities to be happy. Seeing someone else doing well serves as a reminder that our lives will turn around too.

AFFIRMATION: Today I will enjoy myself and find happiness in simple things.

May 1

Inner peace can be reached only when we practice forgiveness. Forgiveness is the vehicle for changing our perceptions and letting go of our fears, condemning judgments and grievances.
  —Gerald Jampolsky

Inner peace is the prize. Serenity is the goal. When we achieve these, we are at home within ourselves. We can be alone and not be lonely and afraid. We can be happy and satisfied, regardless of surrounding circumstances. We feel grounded, regardless of the winds that swirl around us.

We reach forgiveness by realizing that others have done the best they could, given their fears and limitations. The same is true for us. Everyone's capabilities are not the same, and we all create different standards for ourselves.

If we can forgive ourselves, realizing that no one is perfect, it becomes possible to forgive others.

AFFIRMATION: Today I'll monitor my thoughts and attempt to eliminate the negative ones about myself and others.

May 2

Mentally rehearse handling potentially difficult situations in which negative emotions might be triggered in the future. See, hear and feel yourself handling the situation easily until you've conditioned yourself with a sense of certainty that you can confidently and powerfully deal with anything that occurs.
  —Tony Robbins

Many sports teams—Olympic and professional—use visualization to picture success under their most stressful circumstances. Coaches teach their athletes to picture, over and over again, every move being completed perfectly in their minds long before the actual event.

Mental rehearsal can help when we anticipate a difficult conversation, when we need to do something we haven't done before, or before negotiating an important issue. We can practice in advance by visualizing ourselves as calm, able, intelligent and savvy.

AFFIRMATION: Today I will visualize myself handling a difficult situation with ease and confidence.

May 3

Re-evaluate your potential.

We all have more potential than we use. In fact, with our Higher Power's support, we are virtually unlimited. For every problem, there is a solution. We can create new abilities—go back to school, read, practice, talk to people.

Too often we limit ourselves by thinking "I could never...." Perhaps in the past we have let another person define our abilities and have been undermined.

We all have more ability than we give ourselves credit for. To actualize potential, we just have to be willing to take the first step and the next, and the next. We develop by being willing to take the next step. Just because we haven't done something before now, doesn't mean we can't do it!

AFFIRMATION: Today I will think about the abilities I have yet to develop and take a step toward developing one.

May 4

Will you take good care of yourself today?

If we don't take good care of ourselves, who will? Some of us think that self-care is self-ish. NOT TRUE! Taking good care of ourselves is a gift to others. To be a good parent, to do well on the job, we must be in good physical, mental and emotional health.

If we adopt a martyr role and are always sacrificing ourselves, we make everyone else feel guilty and we stay miserable too. If, on the other hand, we are happy and peaceful, we affect others in a positive way. Physical, mental and emotional health are worthy goals. We deserve them.

AFFIRMATION: Today I will take responsibility for taking care of myself. I will rest when I'm tired, eat when I'm hungry and call a friend if I'm lonely.

May 5

There are three excellent reasons for becoming a less aggressive driver. First, when you are aggressive, you put yourself and everyone around you in extreme danger. Second, driving aggressively is extremely stressful. Your blood pressure goes up, your grip on the wheel tightens, your eyes are strained, and your thoughts are spinning out of control. Finally, you end up saving no time in getting to where you want to go.
—Richard Carlson

I was in three accidents during the time I was going through my divorce—fortunately none were serious. When we are upset and distracted, an accident is more likely, so it's wise to take it easy in the car.

Whenever possible, let's give ourselves the gift of extra time for travel so that we don't add unnecessary stress to our day. It's easier to be patient when there's extra time.

AFFIRMATION: Today I will give myself extra time for travel and notice how my stress level is affected.

May 6

Infinite gratitude for the past
Infinite service in the present
Infinite responsibility for the future
That is Zen.   —Huston Smith

If we become grateful for our experience, reach out to others and take responsibility for creating our lives from now on, we will find peace.

We may not be there yet, but the state is worth working toward, for then our lives will be in our hands.

AFFIRMATION: Today I will contemplate the limitless possibilities of my life.

May 7

Talk is cheap.

Don't make promises unless you know you can keep them. This is especially true with children. It's easy to say something in the moment to make everyone feel good, but overall, breaking promises does damage to everyone.

Don't let a mood determine whether you'll make or keep a promise or appointment. Nothing breaks trust more than not following through on your word.

AFFIRMATION: Today I will think carefully before I make a promise.

May 8

I sidestep other's negativity.
My peace of mind lies in not becoming defensive.
I protect myself in negative situations. —Sue Patton Thoele

It's easy to get caught up in someone else's state of being, especially during divorce, when we react with intensity toward one another. We need to remember that we are responsible for our own states. If we become defensive in reaction to someone else's action, we enter into their state. This is our choice.

We don't have to go there. We can always take a "time out" and choose to discuss the issue when the other person is calm. I did all my negotiations on the phone because I knew I could hang up if things got out of control.

Reading something positive in the morning helped me set my state for the day and reminded me that my state of mind was my own responsibility.

AFFIRMATION: Today I will do what I can to avoid a pessimistic state of mind. I will read, take a walk outside or take a break when necessary.

May 9

Life is what happens… while we are busy making other plans.
—Pablo Neruda

In other words, it doesn't pay to worry. What we think will happen doesn't, and what we don't expect does. If we are all worn out from worrying about something that never happens, we won't have the energy or creativity to deal with what actually occurs.

There's a difference between being responsible and being a worrier: the first empowers and the other disables.

AFFIRMATION: Today I will ask my Higher Power to help me with my anxieties. I will practice not worrying about *anything* for an hour.

May 10

Listen—with your eyes, heart and mind, as well as with your ears.

Eighty percent of communication is non-verbal. Pay attention to what is being said in all ways. Note body language, tone of voice and the vibrations coming from the person. How is that affecting you? What is your reaction to what you observe?

This is important information in the negotiation process. Take in as much information as you can because this influences how you make decisions.

AFFIRMATION: Today I will practice active listening in all my encounters.

May 11

Loving is doing. —Florie W.

This statement implies that people don't know we love them unless we act accordingly. This simple truth is often overlooked.

AFFIRMATION: Today I will look for opportunities to reach out and perform a loving act for someone I care about.

May 12

Live so that you wouldn't be ashamed to sell the family parrot to the town gossip. —Will Rogers

Or, what if, like Jim Carrey's character in the movie *The Truman Show*, our lives were lived in front of a camera and broadcast all over our world? What would we want others to see?

This is the criteria that, when lived by, gives us peace. We don't have to be perfect, just acceptable—to ourselves, most of all.

AFFIRMATION: Today I will review my recent behavior to see if there's something I need to change.

May 13

Things which matter most must never be at the mercy of things which matter least. —Johann Wolfgang Van Goethe

We must choose our battles wisely. When we find ourselves embroiled in an issue which isn't really important, we need to try to let it go. If we show cooperation to another person, we are more likely to receive cooperation when we need it. If we are parents, as the future unfolds there will be many occasions for contact with the other parent. If we are flexible, it's likely that we will receive greater cooperation in return.

When it comes to shared parenting, what matters the most is the *execution* of agreements, not the agreements themselves. Keeping the lines of communication open, mutual consideration, respect and flexibility make the difference between stress- or peace-filled lives.

The well-being of our children and ourselves matters. The well-being of our former partner matters too. If our partner is providing financial support, we want that support to continue. If he or she is miserable and unable to keep a job, we will suffer financially too. If our partner is raising our children, we need to be concerned for her or his well-being. We want our children's caregivers to be in good health, both mentally and physically.

AFFIRMATION: Today I'll put first things first.

May 14

Write down all the reasons why you love each person you relate with. Then, when the going gets tough, take the list out and reread it. It resolves problems quickly. —Leo Buscaglia

During difficult times, our perspective may become unbalanced. When we are shaky emotionally we may take offense or feel rejected by someone who doesn't mean to hurt us. Our children are shaken as well, and arguments may escalate out of sheer fright and worry.

Balance is achieved by recognizing and acknowledging what we like in a person in addition to what makes us angry. This is important to practice with those we love and to whom we do not want to cause further harm.

AFFIRMATION: Today I will write down all the reasons I love each person in my life.

May 15

Today I claim the gifts forgiveness gives. —A Course in Miracles

Forgiveness at the end of a relationship is a tall order. Often, particularly in the early stages, it seems impossible, but asking for God's help in achieving the state of forgiveness makes it possible time.

Why do we want to forgive? Because holding onto anger and resentment is bad for us. It causes stress and illness and gives us wrinkles and ulcers. One way to achieve forgiveness is to realize that we aren't perfect and that no one else is either. We are judged by how we judge others, and are trapped in the past by holding onto resentment and grudges.

We forgive because we want to move on and we want our power back. We want to live in the present and for the future, not in the past.

AFFIRMATION: Today, by understanding that I'm not perfect, I can let go of the imperfections in others.

May 16

Live your life so that the preacher won't have to lie at your funeral. — Taken from a temple library wall

When all is said and done, how would we like to be remembered? When friends are speaking to our children, what would we like them to hear? What would we like our friends to say to each other about us?

In the aftermath of a breakup, will we be the one who rises above difficult circumstances with our integrity intact or will we remain bitter and vengeful? Will our family be proud of us and the way we were able to rise above the ordinary and go for the great?

AFFIRMATION: Today I will live my life in a way to ensure that I'll be missed when I'm gone.

May 17

An hour spent fishing adds a day to your life. —John McMahon

Being on the water, in quiet, perhaps in solitude, surrounded by a peaceful vista soothes the soul and calms the nerves. This is taking care of ourselves. If you don't fish, take a book to read or a drawing pad and give yourself some peace and connection to Mother Earth.

In stressful times we need to take time to replenish ourselves. Reducing stress really does add days to our lives.

AFFIRMATION: Today I will make plans to sit in nature and let it restore me.

May 18

"Which would drive you more: keeping someone from stealing $100,000 you'd earned over the last five years, or acting on an opportunity to earn $100,000 in the next five years?"
—Tony Robbins

So much energy and time—sometimes years and years— are spent fighting over assets, each party trying to prove his or her needs are greater than the other's. Why not share assets and spend time creating ways to develop more instead of fighting about what there is now?

In a fight we end up with fewer assets than we would have had by cooperating in the first place. Lawyers fees are high, we lose time, energy and our health suffers from the stress we experience. Is a battle worth all that?

AFFIRMATION: Today I will think about ways I might minimize, rather than exacerbate, the negotiations of my divorce, for everyone's sake.

May 19

We must be willing to get rid of the life we planned so as to have the life that is waiting for us. —Joseph Campbell

I have a friend who, when his wife left him, and because of some other problems, found life overwhelming and took an overdose of medication. He was found by a neighbor who called an ambulance and saved his life.

He spent a month in the hospital. When he got home he found a piece of mail that informed him he had won a major award for his writing. He won a substantial sum of money, an all-expenses-paid retreat at a writers' colony and an opportunity to read his work in a prestigious venue. He almost missed a chance to receive the appreciation and recognition that he had earned.

He had assumed his life was over. He was wrong. He's living on the water on the East Coast, teaching college and has had at least three books published since he attempted to end his life. We never know what's waiting for us just around the corner.

AFFIRMATION: Today I will recognize that my Higher Power has many good things in store for me. I am willing to be an open and receptive vessel for them.

May 20

Your work is to discover your work and then with all your heart give yourself to it. —Buddha

Divorce is a gateway to a new reality. Many opportunities present themselves at this time. When one door closes, another door opens, so be alert. Sometimes our real work is not what we will be paid for. Some of us have to work at a job to earn a living, but our real work is elsewhere. If we can't do what we really want to do right now for money, we can do it on a volunteer basis.

My real work began after my divorce as a volunteer. When I knew what I wanted to do I went back to school to complete a bachelor's degree, got an M.S.W. and have written two books. Before my divorce I never would have dreamed that this was possible.

AFFIRMATION: Today I will think about the kind of work I can give my whole heart to, and if I'm not already doing it, I will take a step in that direction.

May 21

Here is a test to find whether your mission on earth is finished—if you are alive, it isn't. —Richard Bach

Many of us mistakenly think that after we separate, our lives are over. I am happy to tell you that this is *not true*! Life as we knew it may be over, but another life is just beginning. It's up to us to define what we want in our new situation.

The future depends on our attitude now. If we choose to cling to the past, tempting as that may be at times, we will miss our own boat to the future. We are all capable of much more than we know now. Our Higher Power has wonderful things in mind for us. Be open to growth and new ideas. All things are as they should be.

AFFIRMATION: Today I will stay open to new ideas and possibilities, so that I may come to understand what my Higher Power has in store for me.

May 22

Forgiveness is a thought, not a behavior. It is an inner expression of self-respect and integrity. The grounds for forgiving are simple: grievances are unworthy of you. —Hugh Prather

To harbor resentment against others is to diminish ourselves. When we allow negativity to reside in our minds, we reduce our creativity and the connection to what will heal us. Negative thoughts are natural and are often a response to being provoked, but when we allow them to take over our day, we give them power. Resentment is like a snowball rolling downhill. As it rolls, it gets larger and larger, taking up more and more room in our minds.

Forgiveness doesn't mean that we agree with or condone a behavior. It means that we accept the situation and choose to let resentment go. Grievances will keep us from our destiny. We have better uses for our energy.

AFFIRMATION: Today I realize that holding a grudge diminishes me and I want to enhance my self-respect, not reduce it.

May 23

We have a tendency to judge ourselves by our intentions and others by their actions. —Alex Gutterman

Isn't this true? We know what our own intentions are, but we are not aware of others', unless we ask them. When we are upset we are much more reactive than when we are calm, which means we may jump to conclusions. We may escalate hostility or, conversely, act naïvely based on only half the story.

It's always wise to get clarification, if possible. If we understand others' motives, we will be in a stronger position to choose our next action accordingly.

AFFIRMATION: Today I will make an attempt to understand a situation fully before reacting.

May 24

A good friend will sharpen your character, draw your soul into the light, challenge your heart to love in a greater way.
—Unknown

A good friend will tell you the truth and will do it in a way that does not destroy you or the friendship. Seek out people who will be supportive without coddling you too much. Those who only agree with us can't help us see the truth, and those who are always critical can't show us the light.

AFFIRMATION: Today I will be grateful for my friends.

May 25

Learn to get in touch with the silence within yourself and know that everything in this life has a purpose. —Elisabeth Kubler-Ross

It's difficult to have a perspective of the big picture while going through major change because daily survival uses up a lot of our energy. However, know this: divorce and the pain you feel will serve a higher purpose in your soul's development. Your higher purpose is coming and will be revealed to you. You are being prepared for something greater.

Many who were once devastated by the end of a relationship have gone on to new and more satisfying lives. You can too. Meditate. Ask your Higher Power for the help you need. Get quiet and listen for the answer.

AFFIRMATION: Today I will sit in silence for 20 minutes and ask God for insight into my situation.

May 26

Perfectionism is the voice of the oppressor, the enemy of the people. It will keep you cramped and insane your whole life. —Anne Lamott

One of the moods or stages of divorce that seems to go on forever is the "I coulda-shoulda-woulda." We look back, examine and judge ourselves. We think and rethink everything. While examining our half of the responsibility is good and important, it's also important to understand that perfection in a human being is impossible. Realizing this makes it possible to forgive ourselves and others. It may not be easy, but it's possible.

If we expect perfection from ourselves, we will not be able to take risks. Making mistakes won't be an option, so we'll stop ourselves from trying something new. If we aren't willing to try new things, we will remain stuck in unhappiness because we can't stay in the old ways either. Don't stop yourself from expansion because you are afraid of not being or looking perfect. It will make you feel cramped and crazy. Trying out new ideas gives us hope for the future, as long as we aren't too hard on ourselves.

AFFIRMATION: Today I will stop myself from being self-critical. I will give myself permission to make mistakes while I learn.

May 27

When you see only two alternatives—yours and the other one—look for a third alternative. —Stephen R. Covey

What is often overlooked in relationships in general and in creating separation and divorce agreements in particular, is that if a solution isn't agreeable to both parties, the terms may not be met and the battle continues—and continues. It's much more important to work on the relationship between the parties, because if there is mutual respect, it's much more likely that the terms will be carried out. If war prevails, retaliation escalates, and both parties look for ways to nail the other. Legal fees continue to mount, and the situation goes from bad to worse. This is destructive to the children and to the general well-being of the adults.

In any negotiation there is a third alternative, requiring compromise by both parties, but is usually more fair and therefore more likely to be carried out in the long term.

AFFIRMATION: Today I will be open to a third alternative to further peace in my relationships.

May 28

In matters of style, swim with the current. On matters of principle, stand like a rock. —Thomas Jefferson

In the Twelve Step movement we use the expression "First things first." Some things are not worth arguing about or expending energy on. Other issues are worth holding our ground. Our resources are limited and there's only so much energy to go around. Let's make the distinction and choose our battles wisely.

AFFIRMATION: Today I will differentiate among issues and choose the ones that are the most important, keeping "one day at a time" in mind.

May 29

To be really great in little things, to be truly noble and heroic in the insipid details of everyday life, is a virtue so rare as to be worthy of canonization. —Harriet Beecher Stowe

For those of us who are raising children, there are so many little things— thankless things in the moment—to be done every day. Yet they all are woven into the fabric of our lives. The quality of the quilt is shaped by the little pieces and the effort that we invest in them to create a beautiful uniqueness.

When we wish things were different, we miss the gift of the present. It's important to stay alert to the beauty that surrounds us and enjoy doing the small tasks. In everything we do, our attitude, as in the glass half-full or half-empty perspective, determines what we perceive.

AFFIRMATION: Today I will be as conscious as I can of the good in doing the small, everyday things in life.

May 30

"The ultimate measure of a person is not where he stands in the moments of comfort and convenience, but where he stands at times of challenge and controversy." —Martin Luther King, Jr.

Divorce is a time of ultimate challenge. There are times when we are stretched to the limit of endurance.

We must ask ourselves what kind of example we wish to be for others. Do we just talk a good game or do we walk the talk?

AFFIRMATION: Today, even in times of challenge, I will act on my principles and not allow myself to react to negative stimuli.

May 31

You cannot plow a field by turning it over in your mind.
—Unknown

There are times when thinking is simply not enough and we have to make a move. Procrastination, rumination and paralysis are the enemies. One move usually generates another, but we have to start somewhere.

AFFIRMATION: Today I will take action on some things I have been procrastinating about, starting with the easiest ones first.

June 1

Decide what you want, decide what you are willing to exchange for it. Establish your priorities and go to work. —H.L. Hunt

We can achieve almost any goal by taking the steps mentioned in the quotation above. Where most of us falter is in accepting that we have to give something up to achieve what we want. If we want to have money in the bank, we can't spend it all. If we want to lose weight, we need to eat less. If we want to be happy, we can't depend on others to make it happen. If we want to reach a compromise, we have to be willing to give something up ourselves.

We may only have to give up our time or our money, but sometimes it's both. In order to become independent, we have to give up dependency. Are we willing to give up something to achieve a goal?

AFFIRMATION: Today, as I look at a goal, I'll determine what I have to give up to accomplish it and ask myself if it's worth it.

June 2

I am no longer afraid of storms, for I am learning to sail my own ship.
—Louisa May Alcott

Storms are a part of life. They come, wreak havoc and are gone. Divorce is one of the worst emotional storms there is, so if we choose our reactions wisely and manage the crisis well, we will come out of it a stronger and wiser person. We will also have been a good example for our children.

We can set an intention today to do things in an upstanding and rational manner. When we're tempted to do otherwise, our decision to be wise and strong will already be in place.

AFFIRMATION: Today I realize that I've grown stronger because of what I've been through and although it's been painful, I appreciate my new strength of character.

June 3

Only a decision is required to change one's mind. —Harry Palmer

Instead of spending time worrying about others' choices, thoughts and behaviors, we can focus on our own. This puts us in the driver's seat of our lives.

If we've acted badly, we can apologize. If we find out we were wrong, we can admit it. If we're not happy in a job, we can look for another one. If we've stopped doing a hobby, sport or craft that we love, we can take it up again or try a new one.

We can change the way we think and go with the flow. We don't have to be locked into a particular way of living. There's a big world out there, and it offers many, many possibilities.

AFFIRMATION: Today, if I find myself thinking that there's only one way, I will be open to the possibility that there may be more avenues to choose from.

June 4

We may have to give up who we were in order to become who we're g ing to be.

Most people fear change. We don't like the unfamiliar and are uneasy in new circumstances. *But* this doesn't mean that change isn't good or at least won't feel better after time has passed. Divorce can be a gateway to our own potential, and sometimes the familiar must be discarded in order to create the new.

If we are stuck with the circumstance of a breakup or divorce, we can choose to hold on to the past and be a victim or we can choose to let the past go and get on with creating our own lives—and be brilliant!

AFFIRMATION: Today I am willing to think about how I can get to be who I really am—not as part of a relationship, but as my own unique and wonderful self. I will ask my Higher Power to guide my discovery.

June 5

Great minds discuss ideas; average minds discuss events; small minds discuss people. —Unknown

Our natural tendency, during separation, is to discuss people—what an ex did or didn't do or say, what in-laws had the nerve to do, what friends did and so on. This mode gets us nowhere. It weighs us down. Venting is good and necessary, but let's not do it longer than necessary. Ideas are more interesting to everyone.

Read as much as you can, even if it's only a few pages a day. We get ideas from books and classes. Get information from good sources. Talk to interesting people you know and ask about what they are doing. Fill yourself with new knowledge.

AFFIRMATION: Today I will read something in one of my areas of interest to gather new ideas for my life.

June 6

God gives every bird its food, but He does not throw it into its nest. — Unknown

It's important to understand that our ultimate well-being is up to ourselves and God. There are no guarantees in life, as the statistics on divorce prove.

Working hard and asking a Higher Power for help is an unbeatable combination. Initially it may be difficult to believe we will be all right financially—but this is an opportunity to develop our unlimited potential and unearth new abilities and strengths of our own.

Parents, of course, have an obligation to be financially responsible for their children. Food, clothing, shelter and nurturing are children's basic rights, so both mom and dad need to do the best they can to provide them.

AFFIRMATION: Today I will use my imagination to uncover some of my untapped potential and ask my Higher Power's help in developing new abilities.

June 7

Beautiful young people are acts of nature, but beautiful old people are works of art. —Unknown

Let's work on becoming beautiful old people now. If we are lucky enough to grow very old, let us have the luxury of wonderful memories to look back on. Let's not allow bitterness to linger beyond its time and carve down-turned, permanent grooves of sadness into our faces. We need to protect our future, elderly selves by preparing financially as best we can—and we also need to create a savings account of wonderful times to look back on.

Connection with our Higher Power, the result of spiritual development now, will be important to our sense of safety and well-being as our lives become more and more restricted by physical limitations.

To be the kind of person that others want to visit and to grow old with, to embody grace and dignity, to be a gentle advisor to the next generation is to become a work of art.

AFFIRMATION: Today I will either make a memory, or make plans to make one, so I can think about it later and smile.

June 8

Call an old friend.

There's nothing like a heart-to-heart conversation with a trusted old friend: someone who knew you "way back when...", who knew your faults and liked you anyway.

Talking to a person from the past is reassuring. It defines a context for what is happening now. We had a life before, we have one now, and we will go on after all this is over.

AFFIRMATION: Today I'll call someone who will be happy to hear from me because we haven't spoken in a long time.

June 9

Seek out that particular mental attribute which makes you feel most deeply and vitally alive, along with which comes the inner voice that says, "This is the real me." When you have found that attribute, follow it. —William James

The more we know about our own actions, reactions, thoughts, abilities, feelings, denials and what we tend to avoid, the better off we are. Self-exploration is critical now as we attempt to create a new life. We can't know ourselves too well.

Who is the real you? What makes you feel vitally alive? Only we can answer those questions. No one can do it for us, nor can we do it for anyone else. Joy is present in this exploration because it's a pursuit of our real calling, of what we are meant to contribute to the world. Each of us has a particular attribute or a particular combination of talent, experience and knowledge that is highly valuable to others. If we haven't found it yet, keep looking—it's there.

AFFIRMATION: Today I will explore what makes me feel deeply and vitally alive and if I find it today, I will acknowledge and celebrate it.

June 10

This is the single most powerful investment we can ever make in life—investment in ourselves, in the only instrument we have with which to deal with life and contribute. —Stephen R. Covey

Many of us resist making an investment in ourselves. We give a lot to others and may have been taught that it's selfish to invest in ourselves. Nothing is farther from the truth. If we aren't taking care of ourselves, who will? We need enough to eat, we need to rest, we need to have our teeth taken care of regularly and to see a doctor when we're ill. We need to take classes and read good books. We need friends and family. We need money to live on. We need relaxation. We need to laugh.

Make sure that you are investing in yourself while you are investing in others. Be sure to nurture yourself—you'll be better for others if you do.

AFFIRMATION: Today I will make an investment in me.

June 11

Learn from the mistakes of others. You can't live long enough to make them all yourself. —Unknown

Listen and learn. Some of the best ways to avoid mistakes in divorce are to read, join a group and talk things over with someone you trust before making big decisions. There is a great deal of information and wisdom out there. Why not avail ourselves of it to save our sanity, time and money?

Many people have been through this experience before us and we can learn from them. Choose someone you think went through their divorce well and talk to them about how they did it.

Join a support group. Spending time with people who are going through the same ordeal helps us feel normal and understood, and we pick up "do's and don'ts" by listening to others' stories.

AFFIRMATION: Today I will find some support for myself.

June 12

To keep a lamp burning, we have to keep putting oil in it.
—Mother Teresa

With the extra responsibility we take on during divorce it's all too easy to neglect our physical and mental health.

One way to begin the day with some positive energy is to make it a practice to read some uplifting material. Find books that offer positive thoughts or spiritual inspiration and read a little every day. Have a collection of music for the car: calming, upbeat and inspirational choices are good because they help alter our mood on the way to or from work, or while we're doing errands.

Eating nutritious meals also helps us in many ways. We'll have more energy, think more sharply and even look better. Many of us eat when we're stressed, but eating junk starts a downward cycle. Choose the food with the best nutrition available.

AFFIRMATION: Today I will assemble a collection of uplifting materials and make healthy food choices. This will enhance my self-esteem.

June 13

Perform an anonymous service.

Performing a service without expecting something in return benefits the recipient and is a gift to ourselves as well. There is internal joy and satisfaction in helping others because this is how God works in the world. He sends us to each other.

We will not know how far a simple act of kindness may go, because it's passed on from one person to the next as our recipient does something for someone else, or talks about what happened. We will also be blessed at some point because surely what we send out will come back to us.

AFFIRMATION: Today I will plan to do something nice for someone else and do it anonymously.

June 14

Choose being kind over being right. —Richard Carlson

Our egos tell us we must be right. Being right gives us illusory power over another. To prove we are right we need to argue and rationalize our opinion and drive the point home. Why is this so important? Precious energy is expended; we are depleted. And isn't it possible that others are hurt by the hammering?

When feeling the need to be right, think about how you may feel about this next week. Will the animosity generated by proving ourselves right be worth it? As asked in *A Course in Miracles,* "Would you rather be right or happy?"

AFFIRMATION: Today I will choose being kind over being right and feel the difference in my emotional state.

June 15

The conflict between what one is and who one is expected to be touches all of us. And sometimes, rather than reach for what one could be, we choose the comfort of the failed role, preferring to be the victim of circumstance, the person who didn't have a chance.
—Merle Shain

The opportunity to make lemons into lemonade looms large at the end of a relationship. We have a momentous choice to make that influences all other decisions to follow. Will we choose to go through the breakup as a victim and remain stuck in the past or will we decide to use it as a catapult to propel us into the future where many opportunities await us?

Breaking up feels like a rollercoaster ride with our moods and attitudes changing often, but if our global decision is to make the best of the situation, we will be far better off than if we choose to be a victim. What will our choice be?

AFFIRMATION: Today I will do an attitude check and if I have chosen to be a victim, I'll think about ways to turn myself around.

June 16

Coincidence is God's way of remaining anonymous. —Unknown

Some of us believe that there's no such thing as "coincidence," but instead a Higher Power or Universal energy is at work. Coincidence may not be random at all.

We may ask God for help and sometime later, help arrives. A friend calls at just the right time. Unexpected money arrives when we need it the most. We find a person or the information we were seeking, even though it was like finding a needle in a haystack. Do we doubt at that point? Instead of believing that our prayers have been answered, do we assume "It's just a coincidence, God doesn't really answer prayers"?

God answers prayers by sending us to each other. Let's ask for guidance and watch for miracles.

AFFIRMATION: Today I will ask for help and guidance. My faith will grow as my prayers are answered.

June 17

I've learned that you shouldn't go through life with a catcher's mitt on both hands. You need to be able to throw something back.
  —Andy Rooney

To expect to receive without giving is unrealistic. To expect others to compromise and not expect it of ourselves is childlike. Only immature people expect to have everything go their way. What's more, if we don't do our share of compromising, we will get less consideration from others in the long run. We need to do our part.

Conversely, we don't have to take on more than our share. We need to be able to throw back what doesn't belong to us.

AFFIRMATION: Today I will examine my expectations of myself and others.

June 18

Most of the time when we are blocked in an area of our life, it is because we feel safer that way. We may not be happy, but at least we know what we are—unhappy. Much fear of our own creativity is the fear of the unknown. —Julia Cameron

When we leave a long-term relationship, it's usually because we have been unhappy. After it ends it's not unusual to feel very uneasy, unsure and uncomfortable. Sometimes we think we have made a mistake because we are *so* uncomfortable. The discomfort arises from the loss of the old way of life when we haven't created the new one yet. This stage is part of the separation process.

Now is the time to pull out all the stops. We are redefining ourselves and our new lives. We need to look at all our possibilities and pursue those that appeal to us.

AFFIRMATION: Today I will try something new and explore my creativity.

June 19

Too many people overvalue what they are not and undervalue what they are. —Malcolm Forbes

An illusion that occurs during and after the ending of a relationship is that everyone is okay but us. When we're having a bad day, we may get upset at the sight of a family at the store or on the street and ask ourselves, "Why couldn't that be me?" We may feel sad and wish things were different.

While this is natural, it's much better for us to focus on who we are now, where we want to go and understanding the steps that will get us there. What have we learned so far? What have we managed well that surprised us? What strengths have we developed? Take a few moments to appreciate how far you have come.

AFFIRMATION: Today I will make a list of all my attributes, strengths and abilities and appreciate them.

June 20

I've learned that even when I have pains, I don't have to be one.
—Unknown

When we are being a pain to others it's like shooting ourselves in the foot. At a time when we need friendship and comfort, we may push people away by acting ungrateful, crabby, annoyed or judgmental. If tempted to act in any of those ways, we need to take a walk, a nap or at least a few deep breaths, so that negativity doesn't spill over onto others.

It's better for us, and our relationships, if we drive ourselves up onto the high road and be as positive as we can. This may be hard to do at times, but we will feel better if we do.

AFFIRMATION: Today I will remember to give myself a time-out if I feel a tantrum coming on. I'll remember to listen and be compassionate.

June 21

When I give my power to another person, it's like letting the waiter eat my dinner. —Love Unlimited

When we rely on others to make decisions for us, to tell us who we are, what to do or how to think, we give our power to that person. When our happiness depends on what other people do or how they think of us, we give more power away.

When we take responsibility for ourselves and the quality of our lives, we take charge. We must not allow other people to define us.

After being part of a couple, we often have to reclaim some of our personal power and learn to be independent again. Psychotherapy, joining a support group and journal writing are options to aid and speed the process. Be patient, the transition takes time.

AFFIRMATION: Today I will look at areas in my life where I might be giving my power away.

June 22

Work like you don't need the money,
Love like you've never been hurt
and dance like no one is watching. — Kathy Mattea

"Are you kidding?" you may ask. Depending on where you are in the process as you read this quote, you may find it's sentiments anywhere from ridiculous to inspirational. This quote is about recovering our passion and interest in life, which fade as we go through shock, grief, turmoil and change. Passion for life returns a little at a time.

Living with passion is an attitude that can be developed as we heal. Our attitude is our own creation so why not create a passionate interest in life?

AFFIRMATION: Today, no matter how badly I may feel at the moment, I believe that my passion for living will return as I heal.

June 23

I think there is only one quality worse than hardness of heart, and that's softness of head. — Theodore Roosevelt

During a breakup there is often a struggle between hardness of heart and softness of head. We may feel that we have to harden our hearts against the other person in order to let go. We may think that to be gentle and non-judgmental shows softness of head.

Hardness of heart feels terrible. We exist in a state of anger and become walled off from the positive energy that may be around us, which leads to depression. We do this to avoid feeling pain and sadness, but it will actually make things worse. This is how divorce becomes bitter—by staying angry and refusing to look beyond the damage we may be doing in the long run.
For parents: We need to understand when children are involved, we will keep a lifetime connection with our ex . Creating a negative atmosphere will affect our lives for a very long time. Let's be wise about how we handle things.

AFFIRMATION: Today I will look beyond the anger to the years ahead, and set a course of peace for myself.

June 24

Worry is like a rocking chair: it gives you something to do, but it doesn't get you anywhere. —Unknown

Worry may be a lifelong habit. It may give us a sense of control to prepare for any eventuality, but it is debilitating because it saps our creativity, inhibits adventure, keeps us from the present moment and robs us of joy.

Every minute spent worrying is wasted. Worry grows. The more we worry, the more we find to fret about. It's a downward spiral. Worry keeps us awake at night and may cause us to eat too much or too little. We may drink or take drugs to turn off anxiety.

Instead, we need to take action to correct the situation. If there is no action to be taken at the moment, we need to divert our attention to something else. Pray, call a friend, read a book, write a novel, paint a picture, read to a child, take a walk, play with the dog, write in a journal. These are far better uses of time, and there are many more.

AFFIRMATION: Today I will create a "Anti-worry Kit" so that I have choices of activities on hand when I need them.

June 25

An optimist may see a light where there is none, but why must the pessimist always run to blow it out? —Michael de Saint-Pierre

Whom would we rather spend time with—a light-hearted person who assumes the best, or a heavy-hearted person who rains on our parade? Notice who children gravitate toward. Who are their favorite relatives, teachers and friends? Chances are they are people who exude optimistic qualities.

After observation we may discover those who always encourage accomplishment are more "attractive" than those who always warn about pitfalls. Let's think about the qualities that these people exemplify and incorporate as many as possible.

AFFIRMATION: Today, even if I'm not feeling my best and can't be optimistic, I will not blow out anyone else's candle.

June 26

If the grass looks greener on the other side of the fence, most likely it's Astro Turf. —Unknown

As we go through the divorce and the subsequent healing process, we may look at couples and families and wonder "Why can't that be me? Why do I have to be alone when everyone else has someone? Everyone looks so happy and I'm lonely and miserable."

It's helpful to remember that we can't know much about anyone from surface appearance. We don't know what goes on behind anyone's closed doors, and we all have problems of some kind to cope with—an illness in the family, caring for an elderly parent or a handicapped child. Maybe a person lost his or her job, and money is a problem. Sometimes we get a number of problems all at once.

Instead of feeling envy when we see happy people, it may be helpful to say a prayer that we too will be happy again and have many more blessings to look forward to in the future.

AFFIRMATION: Today, if I feel envy or resentment about someone's good fortune or happiness, I will ask God to grant me my own blessings and be grateful for those I have now.

June 27

People are lonely because they build walls instead of bridges.
  —Joseph Fort Newton

After a breakup, we may be tempted to cut people out of our lives. We feel angry, resentful and bitter about the disruption in our lives, our routines and our beliefs. We want to stop the pain, so we build walls to protect our hearts. Sometimes this is absolutely necessary. Sometimes it's not, but we may do it anyway. We also might experience being cut off from our partner's family and friends. We may hurt and decide it's safer to stay behind that wall.

We need to be careful about hastily cutting people out of our present life. Some of our friends may not know how to relate to us in our new context, but don't intend to abandon us. We can choose to be patient with them.

Building connections with new friends is important too. Finding single people who are available to share activities or talk things over will reduce loneliness and give us new ideas.

AFFIRMATION: Today I will be open to the idea of making new friends. I will make at least one phone call toward this goal.

June 28

It's better to be alone than to be in bad company.
—George Washington

We need to learn to be alone. Some of us love it and others dread it, but unless we can be alone, we are vulnerable to anyone who happens to come along. If we are desperate for company, we won't make careful choices because we'll be tempted to hook up with anyone at all.

There is a difference between being alone and being lonely. Alone means to be by oneself, taking care of domestic duties, cooking, reading, resting, studying, having hobbies, playing an instrument, listening to music, writing in a journal, taking a walk and taking care of oneself in general.

Lonely means needing company, and there are plenty of antidotes for that. One of the fastest ways to make new friends is to join a support group or an activity group. Notice I didn't say dating/singles group—that's for later, if you need it.

Make plans for the weekend. Have something to look forward to. It needn't be expensive, just fun. Check the local paper for ideas and invite friends to come along.

AFFIRMATION: Today I will make some plans for future weekends and invite people to come along. I'll go by myself, if necessary.

June 29

He who knows others is learned; he who knows himself is wise.
　—Lao Tse

Separation and divorce create enormous change and temporary confusion. It's wise to spend time understanding who we are now and to continue to do that as we evolve. Chaos reigns at times and we need to help our children and other family members through the transition, leaving little time for our own self-examination.

It's still critical, however, to explore activities like journal writing, reading, listening to others' success stories, meditation, taking walks. Until we understand what we want and need, it's unlikely that we'll get it.

AFFIRMATION: Today I will begin to practice self-examination, even if it's just for a few minutes at a time.

June 30

Take a walk.

Walks are good medicine for everything that ails you. Just being outside changes our energy. We are surrounded by different light, sounds and smells and we breathe fresh air. Moving our bodies for a sustained period releases endorphins in the brain, which create a natural mood lift. We gain perspective by being outside. The sun will come up tomorrow, nature's cycles continue, and even if we're feeling bad today, we're reminded that life goes on and that we will go on too.

Walking carves out time to think and can be an alternative mode of meditation. The activity helps our physical state by increasing circulation and oxygen flow to the brain, reducing depression.

All we need is a pair of comfortable shoes. Let's go!

AFFIRMATION: Today I will go outside and take a walk.

July 1

When we walk to the edge of all the light and then take that step into the darkness of the unknown, we must believe that one of two things will happen: there will be something solid for us to stand on or we will be taught to fly. —Unknown

To leave a relationship is to step into the unknown, and in the beginning, it's all darkness. If we've been together a long time, we can't imagine how we will go on alone. Now here's the good news: we are and will be all right. It's hard to believe at the beginning, but it's true. We are a lot more solid than we think, and we can further develop and sustain our foundation by getting help when we need it. Read good, supportive material, join or start a support group, get into therapy for a while.

Divorce is a beginning, not an end. A whole new life will open up and we will be more than okay—we'll learn to fly.

AFFIRMATION: Today I will be open and ready to accept my wings.

July 2

Cultivate simplicity. —Charles Lamb

Twelve Step programs echo this idea with their slogan: "Keep it simple." When we are in a state of turmoil and confusion, it's helpful to meditate on the idea of simplicity and to reduce extraneous activity or unnecessary burdens, including possessions. Clean out as much as you can to create space. When we cultivate simplicity, our thinking becomes clear and focused. Simplicity opens up room for new possibilities.

AFFIRMATION: Today I will spend some time clearing out what I don't need.

July 3

What lies behind us and what lies before us are tiny matters, compared to what lies within us. —Ralph Waldo Emerson

So many of us believe that there is nothing before us because our primary relationship is over. This is why we cling to the past. However, if we choose to explore our own unique capabilities, interests, beliefs, views, deficits and attributes, we will amaze ourselves. It doesn't matter whether we are women or men, whether we are old or young, a genius or not, have money or not—we have unexplored wonders within. If we live to be 120, we will still find new areas to explore.

There are strengths that we don't even know about yet. This is one of the gifts of a new beginning.

AFFIRMATION: Today I trust that I have what it takes to be who I want to be.

July 4

The secret of life is to let every segment of it produce its own yield at its own pace. Every period has something new to teach us. The harvest of youth is achievement; the harvest of middle-age is perspective; the harvest of age is wisdom; the harvest of life is serenity. —Joan Chittister

The harvest of a separation or divorce may be growth and strength or it may be bitterness. We choose to cultivate and nurture either type of seed. There is much to be learned on this journey—compassion for others in pain, learning to let go of control, a closer connection to our Higher Power, becoming more than we thought we could be. Let us allow this segment to yield its gifts as well.

AFFIRMATION: Today I will be open and receptive to what this segment of my life is teaching me.

July 5

If you can't make a mistake, you can't make anything.
  —Marva Collins

In order to move ahead, we have to be willing to make mistakes, yet so often we impose impossible standards on ourselves and then freeze—afraid that we won't measure up to them. Do we expect a baby to learn to walk without falling?

Perhaps we can learn to accept our own mistakes and become more tolerant of the mistakes of others.

AFFIRMATION: Today I will release the impossible standards I have imposed on myself and others, and lighten up.

July 6

Everything is inside you. Increase and enhance this awareness;
Learn how to become ecstatic inside yourself.
The one you are looking for is you.
The one you want to attain is you. —Swami Muktananda

The truth is that if we aren't happy, no one will *make* us happy. We are responsible for our own happiness and contentment. Once we can make ourselves happy, we naturally become more independent. We no longer depend on others for feelings of well-being. Being happy is our job and our responsibility.

To find our authentic selves, to recognize who we really are, is an ecstatic experience. We may have been taught to hide our true selves because we may not have met someone else's expectations. As children, our true selves may never have been validated. The truth is that we are marvelous. Let's decide to be as genuine as we possibly can be.

AFFIRMATION: Today I will examine the notion of "the real me" to determine what I might have to offer the world. Self-discovery is the way to happiness.

July 7

There are only two states: love and fear.

All states are derived from two: love and fear. Love feels good and fear doesn't. When we are angry, hostile, demanding or upset, it's usually because we are afraid our issues are not being considered. In turn, we seek to protect our interests. This is the normal operating mode of divorce.

When we are caring, considerate, kind, supportive and generous we are operating from the love state. This feels better than fear, although it's not as common as we go through divorce.

While we need to protect our families and be sensible, it helps to get into a loving state as often as possible. Love heals. While a marriage may be over and romantic love isn't present in the moment, there are still plenty of opportunities to give love. It's up to us to find them. All too often, we cut ourselves off from opportunities that life provides because we are upset and depressed. By doing volunteer work, supporting a friend, spending time with one of our children—just to be with them, not to lean on them—or by caring for animals, for example, we can be in touch with love and draw it in to ourselves for healing.

AFFIRMATION: Today I will find a way to express my love to others.

July 8

The brook would lose its song if you removed the rock.
   —Unknown

Isn't it true that we tend to coast when things are going well? We do our jobs, raise our children, work around the house, dwell in our routines. It may be satisfying, not so good or really bad, but it's familiar. We might even justify our complacency by thinking about how we are so much better off than others.

The end of a long-term relationship (a *big* rock) pushes us into development that probably would not have occurred without it. We have to become more conscious parents and develop new skills like managing finances and dealing with household duties and emergencies. We learn to look within for comfort when it's too late to call someone else. We develop a higher degree of empathy for our fellow humans.

So although a breakup might be excruciating, it carves us into stronger, more compassionate and capable people. Our songs are stronger, deeper and more intricate.

AFFIRMATION: Today I will recognize how my song has been enhanced by the rocks in my stream bed.

July 9

There is a time in the life of every problem when it's big enough to see yet small enough to solve. —Mike Leavitt

One challenge we face during a breakup is maintaining perspective. We may shift back and forth between minimizing and catastrophizing—something like "It's really not such a big deal" to "My life is *over* and I'll never be the same again!" This kind of vacillation is a normal part of the process of separation as we attempt to adapt to the new situation.

It's useful to recognize that this will happen at times, and if we feel like we're in one of these extreme modes, it's wise not to make major decisions until we regain our perspective.

AFFIRMATION: Today, if I feel like my perspective may be skewed, I'll talk with someone else to help me regain balance.

July 10

Just for today I will be happy…. Just for today I will try to live through this day only, not to tackle my whole life problem at once. I can do things for twelve hours that would appall me if I had to keep them up for a lifetime. Just for today…
—Sibyl F. Partridge

The way we feel today is not the way we will always feel. When we have a hard day, we know that easier ones are coming—

maybe even tomorrow. If we feel good, let's enjoy that and soak it up.

If we have difficult tasks ahead, they can be handled one at a time. Everything is manageable in small chunks.

AFFIRMATION: Today I will be present, without going back to the past or ahead to the future. I'll do what I can today and let go of the rest.

July 11

We have all been placed on this earth to discover our own path, and we will never be happy if we live someone else's idea of life.
 —James Van Praagh

Many of us have been taught to believe that the reason we are alive is to take care of other people and make them happy. We may have sacrificed our own goals and dreams for another's achievement. During and after a separation we may have to define new dreams and goals.

Deeper recovery comes from taking time to assess what those dreams and goals are and making plans to work toward them. Our Higher Power stands by to inspire and support us in finding our unique path.

AFFIRMATION: Today I will be open to discovery—of my ideas, of my path and what my contribution to the world is to be. I will ask my Higher Power for guidance.

July 12

Whenever you fall, pick something up. —Oswald Avery

Whenever we stretch toward new abilities, we run the risk of falling. In fact, making a mistake is almost guaranteed. Remember learning to ride a bike, playing a new sport or learning to read?

Mistakes are not important. Learning from them is what allows us to make progress toward any goal. We can't develop new skills unless we are willing to trip, pick ourselves up and learn something from the experience. The alternative is paralysis. Which will you choose?

AFFIRMATION: Today I will remember that every mistake is an opportunity to learn and advance. I will practice being fearless about falling.

July 13

I've learned that when you harbor bitterness, happiness will dock elsewhere. — Andy Rooney

When choosing a destination—whether it's a person to talk to, a location for a vacation or a place to live, don't we want a person or place that will make us feel good? Aren't we attracted to warmth, tranquility and compassion?

Bitterness is a common side-effect of a separation or divorce, and most people experience it to one degree or another during this harsh and painful process. However, we don't want to allow it to become a permanent part of our personality. Bitterness creates a cement wall around the heart, and while that serves as a pseudo-protection from pain, it actually disconnects us from compassionate connection with others.

Giving to others is a good antidote to bitterness. Our children need extra attention at this time. Many organizations need volunteers. Perhaps a neighbor has a need we might fill. There are people to be read to, children who need mentoring, animals in shelters who need attention, elderly folks who need help with grocery shopping, people who need assistance learning English or learning to read.

When our hearts are open, and they open up from giving, happiness has a place to dock. This makes life worth living.

AFFIRMATION: Today I will not harbor bitterness.

July 14

Get some sleep—your joy depends on it. One study found that for every hour of sleep sacrificed, people felt eight percent less happy. —O Magazine

Stress, worry and being over-worked and overwhelmed can cause us to neglect the basics. Too often we forget that simple things like getting enough sleep, radically affect our well-being. Rest is important and we must make time for it. Doing so will increase our concentration and our ability to make better decisions, as well as expand our patience and enable us to see the brighter side of life.

On the other hand, if we always feel tired and heavy, regardless of how much sleep we get, these may be signs of depression. If these symptoms persist, get medical attention because there are many things one can do to feel better.

AFFIRMATION: Today I will remember that I am human and that human beings need to sleep to function properly. I will do my best to get the rest I need.

July 15

Once in a while you get shown the light in the strangest places if you look at it right. —Jerry Garcia

Although the ending of a relationship is one of life's most difficult transitions, if we keep our awareness alive we will gain insight that we would not achieve otherwise. When we go through this trial by fire we may become more humble, vulnerable and open than we normally are and therefore can see and feel more than usual. This is actually a gift if we "look at it right," as Garcia suggests.

We can actually take advantage of this opportunity to gain insight, compassion and strength by practicing the Twelve Steps and joining a relationship recovery group.

AFFIRMATION: Today I will be open to insight into myself and others, through my experience. In years to come, I may be grateful for my transformation.

July 16

Talent develops in quiet places, character in the full current of human life. —Johann Wolfgang Von Goethe

Occasionally we may believe that we can do without quite so much character! The current of human life seems like a tidal wave at times, overwhelming and turbulent, leaving us to lie gasping for air on the shore.

It's important to recognize that life goes in cycles: after some really difficult periods, better times follow when we are more able to think about our talents and develop them.

AFFIRMATION: Today I will remember that, while today may not be easy, happier times are sure to come. Life tends to move in cycles.

July 17

It's all right to hold a conversation, but you should let go of it now and then. —Richard Armour

We all want to talk about what's happening in our lives. Our friends and family members do too. When we're in pain or feeling scared, it's easy to become so self-consumed that we have a hard time thinking about anything or anyone else.

Let's remember to show interest and concern for friends and family. It's helpful to be able to talk and share, but it needs to go both ways. Listening to others takes our minds off ourselves, and that shift feels good.

AFFIRMATION: Today I will show others that I care about the events in their lives.

July 18

When written in Chinese, the word "crisis" is composed of two characters—one represents danger and the other represents opportunity. —John F. Kennedy

Crisis always presents opportunity because during times of high stress we are more open to new ideas than when we're in our comfortable routines. Routine can be mind-deadening, but change, even if it's a crisis, can reawaken us.

How do we move from crisis to opportunity? By becoming grateful for what's going right, even in the midst of the turmoil and by being willing to *search* for the opportunity. We can also ask our Higher Power to guide us toward that wisdom.

AFFIRMATION: Today I will actively search for the opportunities that are all around me. I will not let fear of change keep me down.

July 19

When you discover you're riding a dead horse, the best strategy is to dismount. —Lakota saying

Simple? yes. Easy? No!

How often do we strive to make someone into something he or she is not? We may try *everything*: suggesting, nagging, whining, demonstrating, manipulating, crying and temper tantrums—all to no avail.

Sometimes the only thing left to do is let go. Dismount, grieve and walk away.

AFFIRMATION: Today I will decide to use my energy and resources in ways that will be productive in my life.

July 20

Lots of folks confuse bad management with destiny.
  —Kin Hubbard

It's important to be conscious of the little things of daily life, because they shape our destiny. Are we treating our children right? Are we managing money well? When we are afraid, do we hide? Drink too much? Overeat? Take drugs? How are we treating our former partners? Are we reactive, or are we making decisions with the big picture in mind? All of these choices affect our destiny. Do we need to make different choices?

If we recognize destructive patterns in our lives, we can choose to get help. There is no problem too big to be bettered. The sooner we manage our lives well, the better our future will be. Our destiny is in our hands today.

AFFIRMATION: Today I will look at how I manage my life and see if there are improvements I can make for the sake of my future.

July 21

Don't let history control you. —A fortune cookie

At the end of a relationship, it's very wise to examine what went wrong and why. There may be reasons that are subconscious and outside of our awareness. Much of what we believe to be "normal" is what we learned in our family of origin. Our expectations are often shaped by the notions of right and wrong that we learned as children.

For some issues, psychotherapy may be useful. It can help us examine our definition of what we consider normal. For more obvious issues, we can look at past mistakes, learn from them and sidestep repetition in the future.

AFFIRMATION: Today I will start becoming aware of my history so that I don't repeat my mistakes. I'll get help if necessary.

July 22

If you think you're through changing, you're through. —Unknown

When a relationship ends it feels like life is over, and, in truth, the life we knew no longer exists. Change, particularly unexpected change, can be frightening. We may fear that there's nothing left for us because our old life is gone. This is not true.

While change makes us sad and uncomfortable, it also opens a door to our untapped potential. So we have a choice—do we shut down in the face of the unknown, or do we walk ahead, trusting that our Higher Power will lead us into a new life, filled with opportunities, that never would have appeared without this change?

AFFIRMATION: Today I will see change as good and stay alert for the many opportunities that will present themselves in time.

July 23

He who chooses the beginning of the road chooses the place it leads to. It is the means that determine the end.
—Harry Emerson Fosdick

When faced with the complex task of dissolving a marriage, remember that when there are children, you and your spouse will be in a relationship forever. If both parents choose to be in the children's lives, there will be many events where you will both be present. Children will participate in school and religious events, they will graduate, may marry and have children. Even our grandchildren will have events we'll want to attend.

So as we begin the process of separation, we must consider kindness, compassion, respect for the other person and proceed accordingly, keeping the big picture in mind. Even if a partner doesn't act as kindly, our attitude and example will be influential.

AFFIRMATION: Today I understand that the way I behave today will have a strong impact on my future. I will act accordingly.

July 24

The secret to getting ahead is getting started. The secret of getting started is breaking your complex, overwhelming tasks into small, manageable tasks, and then getting started on the first one.
—Mark Twain

When we feel upset or depressed, it's hard to concentrate and easy to become overwhelmed. Life doesn't wait for us to catch our breath. We must focus on our jobs, care for our children, pay our bills and maintain our lives.

Occasionally the difficulty of a task may paralyze us into inaction. Making a list of the steps we need to take, starting with the easiest and crossing it off the list, can motivate us to do the next one. We only have to take one step at a time. Once we get started, our self-image improves and one thing leads to another.

AFFIRMATION: Today I will take one step toward my goal.

July 25

If one does not understand a person, one tends to regard him as a fool.
—Carl Jung

There are always at least two perspectives in a relationship. When we are hurt, it's tempting to lash out at the other person. This is particularly true right after separation.

One of the most difficult tasks at this time and one that requires a high degree of maturity, is coming to understand the other person's perspective. Agreement isn't necessary, but understanding is. Regarding the other person as a fool, or worse, puts us at a disadvantage when attempting to negotiate any kind of settlement or resolution.

AFFIRMATION: Today I will attempt to clarify my thinking by being open to the other person's perspective. I don't have to agree, I just need to understand.

July 26

The longest journey we take is a distance of about one foot—from the head to the heart. —Unknown

We are complex beings and are able to operate on multiple levels simultaneously: intellectual, physical, emotional and spiritual. In our fast-paced world, scrambling to get everything done, we often remain on the intellectual level, taking too little time to integrate the others .

We may wonder why we are still in pain after accepting the fact that we are no longer together as a couple. The divorce or breakup may have been executed, we no longer live with this person and it's over. Why can't we just get over it?

One answer is that we haven't fully integrated this change into our reality, which takes more time than we might expect. "Knowing" something (intellectual) and "accepting" it (emotional) are two different levels of integration. Psychotherapy facilitates the integration of both.

We can experience the physical level by incorporating practices that slow us down, like yoga, meditative breathing, walking outside in nature, or listening to the ocean or meditative music.

We can also access the spiritual level by asking our Higher Power to help us move toward acceptance. Prayer and meditation speed healing.

AFFIRMATION: Today I will take time to move out of the intellectual sphere and to be open to the emotional, physical or spiritual realms.

July 27

The mark of our ignorance is the depth of our belief in violence, injustice and tragedy. What the caterpillar calls the end of the world, the Master calls a butterfly. —Lao Tse

When the end of a relationship comes unexpectedly, it seems that life is over. We grieve. We don't see the big picture.

Every relationship teaches a lesson and adds a dimension to our lives that would not be there otherwise. No relationship is a waste of time. Some will give us gifts and others will teach us what we don't want. Most relationships are a combination of both.

What will we keep to add to the fabric of our experience? What can we learn from this particular person at this specific time? When we look at this situation in the context of our lives as a whole, we will see that it has played an important role in our development.

How will we transform? How will we use this pre-butterfly period?

AFFIRMATION: Today I know that I am on a journey and I'm being transformed. I look forward to emerging as a beautiful butterfly.

July 28

Cowardice is almost always simply a lack of ability to suspend the functioning of the imagination. —Ernest Hemingway

Fear may come and go in waves or hang around a while. What makes fear more powerful is when we become attached to fearful thoughts and allow our imagination to run with them. "What if I spend the rest of my life alone?" What if something terrible happens to my child?" "What if I lose everything and wind up in the streets?" This is called catastrophizing and can be paralyzing.

Allowing ourselves to fill with dread isn't wise. Rampant anxiety can be prevented or reduced by refusing to dwell on all the negative possibilities.

Let's replace frightening thoughts with ideas like: "I am strong and I'll be fine." "I will grow because of this adversity." "People go through this all the time and are okay after a while—I will be too." These statements reflect a more accurate picture of the future.

AFFIRMATION: Today, if I feel fear creeping in, I will replace it with positive thoughts.

July 29

Beyond all thoughts of wrongdoing and rightdoing there is a field. I'll meet you there. — Rumi

In childhood, we were taught about right and wrong, and socialized by our families to get along in the world. In adult relationships, determining right from wrong isn't so easy because we discover that there's more than one way to be right.

Picture a soccer field where the goals on each end represent a different point of view. In a game there is much to be done midfield to bring the interaction to resolution for one side or the other. In human relationships, however, the work done between the two goals must result in a win for *both* sides.

How do we do that? By changing our thinking from "I have to be right" to continuing to work until both people are satisfied. That there are only two solutions—mine and yours— is an illusion. The truth is that there are many possible solutions, so we need to be willing to use our creativity to broaden the options.

AFFIRMATION: Today I realize that there are more than one or two ways to solve a problem. I'll broaden my thinking.

July 30

To live in the present moment is a miracle. The miracle is not to walk on water. The miracle is to walk on the green Earth in the present moment, to appreciate the peace and beauty that are available now. —Thich Nhat Hanh

It seems that we human beings spend very little time in the present moment and have to discipline ourselves to even notice it. Much time is spent lost in memories or worrying about the future, and little is devoted to appreciation of the moment.

Stop. Take a deep breath. Notice what's around you right now. Are you safe? Can you see out a window? Do you have enough food? Do you have a place to live and a bed to sleep on? Do you have reasons for gratitude?

Even though circumstances may be chaotic, we can appreciate the peace and beauty that are available now. As always, we choose our focus.

AFFIRMATION: Today, from time to time, I will notice where I am and realize how lucky I am to be here. I am alive in the moment.

July 31

And as long as space endures, as long as there are beings to be found, may we continue likewise to remain to soothe the sufferings of those who live. —His Holiness the Dalai Lama

The end of a significant relationship causes pain and suffering. It's helpful to recognize that there are many types of suffering— physical, emotional, psychic and spiritual—and there are others who are in pain at this moment. One of the best ways to reduce our own suffering is to be of service to someone else. The opportunities are limitless. An act of love is healing to both receiver and giver, so let's look for ways to be of use. Often there's a person very close to us who would benefit from some loving attention.

AFFIRMATION: Today I will look for opportunities to help another being. In giving this gift, I will also heal myself.

August 1

Keep a green tree in your heart and perhaps the singing bird will come. —Chinese Proverb

When we are in pain, we tend to shut ourselves down in self-protection. The world can look pretty grim at times. While we may be protected from further pain, no light can enter either.

The green tree symbolizes hope. We need to stay hopeful and keep our hearts open, so we attract more light and good things. The more isolated and shut down we are, the darker our world. If we open up, even just a tiny bit, some light will enter, and day by day, we can allow a little bit more until we stand in full light again. The green tree will grow larger and stronger.

AFFIRMATION: Today I will remain hopeful and expectant of good things.

August 2

It is better to sleep on things beforehand than lie awake about them af-terwards. —Baltasar Gracian

When emotions run high and fear is present, we tend to be highly reactive. We "shoot from the lip" and say things we regret later because we haven't monitored our responses.

If we're not sure about what to do next, we can take a break to think. Even if it slows the process, it's better to go slowly and steadily than to have a fast response and regrets later.

For parents: Rather than giving a child an automatic answer of "no," we might say, "Let me think about it." We might find a compromise or if we have to refuse the request, we might do it in a way that teaches the child something.

AFFIRMATION: Today I realize that my words and actions are my responsibility, and I will take time to think before I react.

August 3

But there's more for me to do now
More poems in my head
Young lives for me to nurture
Only one dream old and dead. —Carol Masone

The dream of "happily ever after" is the last thing to die, and we may hold onto that dream long after we know it's over. We may live apart, with papers signed, possessions divided and parenting schedules created; but sometimes when we see our mate again, we just can't believe it's over and that we won't be going back into that relationship.

So we turn our attention to the next task and those who need us. In time, new dreams form and old ones fade.

AFFIRMATION: Today I'll go about the business of taking care of myself and nurturing others, knowing there are more dreams to come.

August 4

People have a hard time letting go of their suffering. Out of a fear of the unknown, they prefer suffering that is familiar.
 —Thich Nhat Hanh

It's marvelous to discover that suffering is optional. There are many circumstances that promote suffering, but do we really have to respond? If someone insults us or acts unfairly toward us, do we have to dwell on it?

Sometimes suffering is so habitual that it becomes a lifestyle. We may forget how to be happy and don't believe that having fun is even possible. Conversation is full of complaint. We must dare to let go of suffering to discover all that life has to offer.

AFFIRMATION: Today I won't allow myself to suffer.

August 5

The secret of joy is the mastery of pain. —Anaïs Nin

Life is a series of ups and downs. Mary Chapin Carpenter sings a song whose lyrics say "Sometimes we're the windshield and sometimes the bug," and we can relate to the bug as a relationship ends.

One element of mastering pain is the recognition that it doesn't last forever. Time itself is a great healer. We have the option of psychotherapy, if necessary, to understand the particular lesson that this relationship has taught us.

Another lesson in mastery is learning to be alone. If we've been in a long-term relationship, being alone may feel frightening, and we may try to fill the void by leaping into another relationship as quickly as possible. We miss a valuable lesson when we choose this path.

As we develop a strong sense of self by not giving in to our neediness, we will know the joy of making decisions from a place of strength. Joy comes from a deep belief that we can handle all the events of our lives—the painful and the joyful.

AFFIRMATION: Today I will consider how to master my pain. I will get help if necessary.

August 6

To risk loving, knowing that loss is inevitable, is the single most important challenge of our lives. —O Magazine

To risk loving, to open ourselves up and let another inside where we are vulnerable, is a monumental decision—especially after we've been dealt a blow. However, what's the alternative?

To give love is a strong human need. When we are shut off, out of touch and not in a state of love, we are protected, but eventually we may dry up like a vegetable that's been left in the refrigerator too long. Loving keeps us juicy.

Yes, there is a risk: our children grow up, our pets die, friends move away, partners sometimes move on, but each relationship has given us a gift. Each relationship has taught us something. Let's learn the lesson, expand our awareness and capabilities, and accept the challenge to keep on loving as much as we can. With time and practice, the risk may seem less threatening. What's the alternative?

AFFIRMATION: Today I will keep my heart open and be loving when I can.

August 7

Those persons are happiest in this restless and mutable world who are in love with change; who delight in what's new simply because it differs from what is old; who rejoice in every innovation, and find a strange alert pleasure in all that is, and has never been before. —Agnes Repplier

It seems that the first reaction to change is fear. Most of us assume that change means "bad," and we resist it. As we all know, the only constant in life is change. Change is inevitable, but we can condition ourselves to look at what's changed from the "glass half-full" perspective and see what we can learn. What good may come of this new occurrence? Where is our blessing in this new situation? A positive attitude brings more positive events into our lives. The opposite is also true.

Positive people attract others. They experience more pleasure and fun. They believe good things are coming their way. We can choose to be positive in most situations and to see the potential present in every situation.

AFFIRMATION: Today, although I may feel sad or angry, I will search for the positive possibilities that exist because I know they are always present. If I don't see them, I'll ask my Higher Power to show them to me.

August 8

Stress is an ignorant state. It believes that everything is an emergency. — Natalie Goldberg

During the breakup of a long-term relationship, our life orientation changes. Our state of mind affects other relationships, our jobs and our children. Stress builds because we are coping with so much change.

An expression used in the Twelve Step movement is "How important is it?" Before we move hurriedly from one task to another, let's stop and assess what's *really* important and take care of those things first. When we do this, it becomes clear that some things take priority. By taking care of the most important issues first, we don't accumulate more stress because we did not attend to them. The less important things sometimes take care of themselves.

AFFIRMATION: Today I will not allow stress to rule my decisions. I will do my best to calm down and make decisions from a centered place.

August 9

Just because you made a mistake doesn't mean you are a mistake.
—Georgette Mosbacher

Are you under the mistaken belief that you have to be perfect? Why do we think that making a mistake lessens our worth? We generally do the best we can, but sometimes can't see the best action to take until later. A mistake doesn't make us a bad person.

Since we aren't perfect, we must accept our own fallibility. When we can admit a mistake and apologize for it, we set ourselves free.

AFFIRMATION: Today I will recognize my mistakes without beating myself up over them.

August 10

No matter the storm, when you are with God there's always a rainbow waiting. —Unknown

When we invite God into our problems, we find solutions. We may forget in times of high stress that God is available to us and will grant us strength and courage when we ask.

Even if a situation is very difficult, when we ask for Divine help, we will see that the outcome is more than we expected, that the result is better than we ever thought possible. New solutions arise.

Some of us make the mistake of blaming God for the actions of another person. We wonder how God could have let this happen to us. The fact is we have free will. God does not control our actions or the actions of others. When we ask for help, however, the blessings of the Divine will help us in more substantial ways than we may have imagined.

AFFIRMATION: Today, even if I can't see it right now, I know there's a rainbow waiting for me on the other side of this hard time.

August 11

I've learned that when you plan to get even with someone, you are only letting that person continue to hurt you. —Andy Rooney

Serenity is the opposite of revenge and is a goal of all Twelve Step programs. When we are serene we are happier, able to be more loving parents, more creative, do our jobs better, enjoy life more.

When we plan to get even, we derive only short-term satisfaction, and then go back to feeling miserable again. If the other person retaliates, there is more revenge to be plotted. We may achieve momentary satisfaction, but we still don't get to happiness. Instead, we find ourselves in a downward spiral of negativity. In a divorce, this becomes an extremely expensive activity.

It's wise to use our limited energy and our resources on positive and constructive endeavors that enhance our well-being.

AFFIRMATION: Today, although I may be tempted, I will not waste my precious energy planning to get even. Instead, I will talk it out with a friend, therapist or group and think about ways to improve my own life.

August 12

If you can't be a good example, then you'll just have to serve as a horrible warning. —Catherine Aird

What would we like our children, family and friends to remember about us as we go through this difficult time? Not many would choose to be remembered as selfish and bitter, a shrew or a bully, or as pathetically weak. We don't want others to say "Boy, I sure don't want to be like *that!*"

Our actions, not our words, demonstrate what we believe is important, and we are sorely tested during times like these. It's not always easy to take the high road but wouldn't we rather have people say "They handled their breakup with mutual consideration and integrity. I wonder how they did it."

We will live with the results of our actions and attitudes for a long time. Let's act in ways we can be proud of. When the dust settles, we'll be glad we did.

AFFIRMATION: Today I choose to set a good example for my children and others.

August 13

Your playing small does not serve the world. Who are you not to be great? —Marianne Williamson

Everyone has something to contribute to the world. Sometimes being released from a relationship is the first step toward greatness. Maybe we are being prepared for an exciting adventure, starting a wonderful new career, developing new strengths, acquiring additional education.

Our world needs all the talent it can get, and we all have a special gift to offer. Our job is to uncover that gift and to be great in our unique way. The world awaits us.

AFFIRMATION: Today I'll look for an opportunity to become more than I am now.

August 14

Far better it is to dare mighty things, to win glorious triumphs, even though checkered by failure, than to rank with those poor timid spirits who know neither victory or defeat.
—Theodore Roosevelt

In other words, don't be afraid to fail. If we let fear rule, our lives become small. We can change this at any time by asking ourselves about what our hearts desire. What do we have to offer the world? Where can we make a difference?

For some of us, it may be in the lives of a few people. For others, it may be working with many. The important thing is that we try, that we are out there living and giving life our best shot.

There is grief work to do after the demise of a relationship but we don't want to remain in that state longer than necessary. Working on ourselves and attempting new endeavors will help us move into our courageous and marvelous next stage of life. Each stage has its own gifts for us.

AFFIRMATION: Today I understand that my life is *not* over because of the end of my relationship. No matter what my circumstances, I know I can improve them.

August 15

Darkness cannot drive out darkness; only light can do that. Hate cannot drive out hate; only love can do that.
—Martin Luther King, Jr.

We have a choice: darkness or light, hatred or love. In which state do we want to exist? Where do we want to spend our days? Our health—emotional, physical and mental—suffers when we choose to stay in darkness and hate. We suffocate our creative gifts and ruin relationships. If we have children, they absorb this state and suffer as well.

By asking a Higher Power to lift us out of the darkness we find relief. We move into a loving state by finding a way to express our caring to another. Children, for example, need love as much as they need food. Might we take some time to nurture a child, a friend, a pet? The act of loving will change our state. *For parents: Anger and hatred are toxic to children. Do your best to be gentle around them.*

AFFIRMATION: Today, despite how I may be feeling, I'll reach out and nurture someone else.

August 16

So often we dwell on the things that seem impossible rather than on the things that are possible. So often we are depressed by what remains to be done and forget to be thankful for all that has been done. —Marian Edelman

This switch in perspective can make the difference between action and depression, anxiety and peace, frustration and happiness, and it's all within our power. Isn't that marvelous?

Most of us have long lists, either in our minds or on paper, that will never be discarded because we keep adding to them. That's a condition of life: always things to do and places to go. When this becomes overwhelming or depressing, an antidote is to write a list of all the things we *have* accomplished. Let's look at the big picture and appreciate all we have completed in the last few years. It's probably pretty amazing.

Loving and encouraging ourselves leads to more of the same. The opposite is also true. *For parents: Acknowledge and appreciate the achievements, kindness and coping abilities of your children, rather than dwell on what still needs to be done.*

AFFIRMATION: Today I'll write a list of all I have accomplished in the past few years and be grateful for all my opportunities.

August 17

The best way to know God is to love many things.
  —Vincent Van Gogh

One of the most painful aspects of separation and divorce is what we perceive as loss of love. We may feel hollow or shriveled up, and the pain may be intense. When we feel this way, we need to look around and find something to appreciate.

Are you in a safe place? Is your chair comfortable? Are your children well? Is there food in your refrigerator? Do you have a bed, a blanket and pillow? Do you know how to read? Do you enjoy music? Do you have a pet or access to one? Are you surrounded by beauty? Do you have a friend who cares about you?

When we feel grateful for what we have, we start the flow of love back into our lives. When we feel that flow, we begin to heal.

The willingness to love many things will help us feel closer to God, and loneliness will be lessened.

AFFIRMATION: Today I'll look for opportunities to express my love and appreciation for the many positive aspects of my life.

August 18

Seek feedback. —Franklin Covey

When Ed Koch was the mayor of New York City, he became famous for asking "How'm I doing?" as he walked around the city. It was a great source of feedback for him.

Ask healthy, trusted adults for feedback. Often we can save ourselves time and money by getting some good advice from experienced people.

AFFIRMATION: Today, if I'm not sure what to do next, I'll ask, listen and learn.

August 19

That the birds of worry and care fly about your head, this you cannot change. But that they build nests in your hair, this you can prevent. — Chinese proverb

At least a million thoughts run through our minds on a daily basis, and they run the gamut from loving and caring to raging and controlling. We choose the ones to attach to and develop.

It's like being in a department store with a wide range of products laid out before us. We decide where to focus our attention. What department are we looking for? Our thought process is similar—we choose to spend time with worry and concern, or encouraging and constructive thoughts.

AFFIRMATION: Today I will spend time with only positive and constructive thoughts.

August 20

I had always thought self-esteem was a state of being. Now I realize it's the constant decision to love myself, regardless of circumstances, all day long. —Mary Casey

Maintaining self-esteem is one of the most difficult challenges we face as we endure the ending of a significant relationship. An example of loving oneself in this context is establishing boundaries that won't allow harmful behaviors. We may opt to walk away from a demeaning discussion, choose not to pursue a relationship that isn't good for us or hold our ground on an important issue with our children.

Other options may include inspiring ourselves with uplifting thoughts from a favorite book, relaxing by listening to music that we love, spending time outdoors or calling a supportive friend. We can also get help from experts when necessary. Self-esteem increases by taking care of ourselves and realizing that we have the ability to do so.

AFFIRMATION: Today I realize that self-esteem doesn't come from the compliments of others, but from my ability to take care of myself.

August 21

The human spirit is virtually indestructible, and its ability to rise from the ashes remains as long as the body draws breath.
—Alice Miller

Isn't this a great thought? Our spirits are indestructible, and we have the ability to come back from just about anything. We may believe we won't bounce back but with time and some recovery work, we can and will revive, and discover even more strengths within us.

We take it one day at a time and do the best we can on any given day—and that doesn't mean perfection. We will rise, gain strength and go on.

For parents: Children need to be told that they can cope and will recover in time. Help them feel hope for the future too.

AFFIRMATION: Today I know that I will rise again and be stronger than before.

August 22

The beads of knowledge are already accepted: it is only necessary to string them together as a necklace. —Ken Wilbur

We often know more than we think we do. Some of our experiences may seem isolated and not relevant to one another, but a closer look at these pieces may allow them to come together and form a body of knowledge that we may not have been aware of before.

When there's a problem to be solved, take a few minutes and write down everything you know about solving it. Think about all the information you already have from various sources. If you find you don't have enough information, get more. Research the Internet, go to the library, talk to people who know about the issue. You will find that you know more than you think. Tackling a problem boosts self-confidence and reduces worry.

AFFIRMATION: Today, rather than worry about a problem, I'll be proactive about solving it, starting with what I already know.

August 23

There has never been a good war or a bad peace.
—Benjamin Franklin

This quote reminds us not to look at a breakup as a reason for battle. Waging war keeps us feeling angry, tense and hostile, undermining our peace of mind and health. Instead, let's get to peacemaking as soon as possible.

AFFIRMATION: Today I will find ways to make peace.

August 24

The past is our cradle, not our prison. The past is for inspiration, not imitation; for continuation, not repetition. —Israel Zagwill

It's important to understand what influence our past had on us, while also understanding that our past is not who we are. We are free to choose differently at any time.

Psychotherapy is a tool that helps us review our past in order to gain an understanding of how it affects the present. We are all influenced by what we learned and accepted as truth when we were children, and some of those "facts" still drive us today. Once uncovered and brought into the light of adulthood, they no longer drive our unconscious mind. We are free to choose different beliefs on which to base our lives.

AFFIRMATION: Today I realize that, if I need to, I can ask for help in order to avoid repeating past mistakes.

August 25

It's easier to go downhill than up, but remember the view from the top is more inspiring. Only those who risk going too far will know how far they can go. —Gennaro Galante

Why allow ourselves to act according to ancient and invalid limitations? Let's not be afraid to go for what we want. Working toward a higher level of existence isn't easy, but increased awareness, even if we fail at first, is worth the effort.

Let's be willing to take a risk and expand our experience!

AFFIRMATION: Today I will move out of the familiar and try something different.

August 26

We don't see things as they are, we see them as we are.
  —Oscar Wilde

While teaching Post-Divorce Parenting classes, instructors are always impressed by how different each person's version of his or her marriage is.

Women are taught in one group and men in another, but each group is taught by the same instructor. Participants answer questions and interact within their group, so instructors hear about the dynamics in each family.

What is interesting is that, although each person is sincerely speaking the truth from his or her perspective, it's usually difficult to match the men with the women in the other class, without looking at names—so different are their stories.

It's possible that the other person's viewpoint is just as "true" as ours, for that person. It's wise to keep this in mind. Understanding our partner's perspective, even if we disagree with it, will facilitate communication and ease any negotiation process, right now and later on.

AFFIRMATION: Today I will try to understand the other side of the story.

August 27

Ninety-nine percent of failures come from people who have the habit of making excuses.
  —God's Little Devotional Book on Success

Ninety percent of excuses are bogus. Making excuses is a failure to commit. Let's choose to be successful.

AFFIRMATION: Today I will not make excuses about anything.

August 28

Anxiety and worry are the parents of temper and disease.
—Unknown

Do you have a collection of activities that help you relax? If not, it's time to develop one. How about sports and exercise? Meditation and accompanying music slow and soothe body and mind. A hobby or craft takes our minds off worries and as does a good book. Laughing at a funny movie is good for the body and soul. If you have friends who make you laugh, add a conversation with them to your list too.

Studies show that people going through divorce or the end of an important relationship have more traffic accidents and get sick more often. We need to be extra careful when we're experiencing high stress.

Rather than fuel worry and anxiety, we need to nurture and take care of ourselves. Let's decide that when feeling tense, we'll do something that will make us feel better as soon as possible. Why not make some plans and have something to look forward to?

AFFIRMATION: Today I will make a list of the various activities that relax me and refer to it when I feel anxious or worried.

August 29

The story of love is not important—what is important is that one is capable of love. —Helen Hayes

We all have been influenced by the Hollywood-style notion of love. We idealize love and wonder why it hasn't worked out for us in that "happily ever after" way. We may be confusing romance with love.

Love is action, not a fleeting feeling that comes and goes, depending on the day and the mood. Love is making the decision to care for a person and demonstrating that caring through action. Giving a sincere compliment, expressing appreciation and affection, helping out when a loved one is sick, bringing home a favorite treat or sharing a favorite activity are all examples of action.

Are we capable of putting another's needs before our own—at least some of the time? We're not talking about martyrdom and constant self-sacrifice, but of giving from the heart. If we are capable of love, we will attract it like a magnet. Love doesn't come on demand, but by attraction. How attractive are we?

AFFIRMATION: Today I will assess whether I am really capable of loving another person.

August 30

Speak life to those who cross your path. The power of words...an encouraging word can go such a long way. May your words be a blessing to someone today. — Unknown

Our words can be an enormous gift to another person. Do you remember someone saying something nice to you and it lifted you for the whole day and maybe longer? Let's pass that gift around.

Children are profoundly affected by what their loved ones say to them. Let's pay particular attention to saying wonderful, supportive things to our children and to young people in general.

AFFIRMATION: Today I will look for opportunities to give sincere compliments to others and give myself extra credit if I can do this for a child.

August 31

I suppose it is tempting, if the only tool you have is a hammer, to treat everything as if it were a nail. —Abraham Maslow

During a breakup or divorce, anger can be a constant companion; and we often react with hostility or sharpness whether it's called for or not. If we have been hurt, it is natural to lash out at the offending person. But that automatic reaction creates more pain and intensifies the crisis.

Anger often masks sadness and fear, so be aware that these emotions probably underlie the anger. This is especially true for men because men have been taught that expressing anger is acceptable, but admitting fear or feeling sad is not.

Is there a better way? How about developing more tools, like listening attentively, flexibility and thinking carefully before saying an automatic "No!" to a reasonable request.

AFFIRMATION: Today I will expand my tool collection.

September 1

When we expand our self-image to include the Soul, we notice a marked shift in our personal consciousness, a liberation from the small egotistical self into a far more spacious context. —Ram Dass

When we allow spirituality to enter our lives, we may see that perhaps there is a reason for our suffering and sadness. Maybe we will use this experience for our development in a larger sense. In ten years, when we look back, we may see that there was an important reason this happened. At the least, people who endure a major loss become more compassionate.

Many have been spurred on to bigger and better things, which would not have happened had their lives remained safe and stable. Let's consider a more spacious context.

AFFIRMATION: Today I will remember that my experience on earth includes the intellectual, physical, emotional and spiritual levels, and I will try to incorporate all levels into my daily existence.

September 2

The roses under my window make no reference to former roses or to better ones; they are for what they are; they exist with God today. There is no time to them. There is simply the rose; it is perfect in every moment of its existence. —Ralph Waldo Emerson

Self-acceptance and being alive in the moment: what simple yet powerful ideas. No excuses, judgments, rationalizations, justifications, self-improvement necessary—just be ourselves, right now.

The flower is. The bee comes.

AFFIRMATION: Today I will find a flower and meditate on its beauty.

September 3

Resolve to be tender with the young, compassionate with the aged, sympathetic with the striving, and tolerant with the weak and wrong... because sometime in your life you will be all of these. —Unknown

As you surely have noticed, life goes on, regardless of what we are going through and how we feel. Decisions have to be made, work has to be accomplished, and relationships continue. We have many roles to fill in our daily lives.

It takes great maturity and discipline to endure the ending of a relationship with grace and to stay in touch with the needs of those around us. When we're loving and compassionate with others, however, we reduce our own suffering.

AFFIRMATION: Today I will resolve to do these things, because without an intention like this, I may not notice the needs of others while I am in pain myself.

September 4

God is absolute truth. I am a human; I only understand relative truth. So, my understanding of truth can change from day to day. And my commitment must be to truth rather than consistency.
—Mahatma Gandhi

When we live in truth, we experience peace. Our responsibility is to live our truth and to search it out when we aren't sure what we believe. Communication is so much clearer when instead of saying "You are wrong!" we say "What's true for me is...." It creates an entirely different tone. Furthermore, *my* truth is a lot more accurate than saying *the* truth is.... Our perspectives change depending on who and where we are at any given time.

A wise person listens very carefully and attempts to understand the other's point of view, which may lead to further expansion or change in his or her perspective.

AFFIRMATION: Today I will resolve to practice one of Stephen Covey's Seven Habits: *Seek first to understand, then be understood.*

September 5

Wisdom is one of the few things in human life that does not diminish with age. Wisdom alone increases until death if we lead examined lives.
—Ram Dass

Those of us who practice the Twelve Steps through a crisis gain wisdom. We learn about ourselves, where our power lies, how to apologize, and gain appreciation for prayer and meditation. This is one way to lead an examined life. The Steps have been used by Alcoholics Anonymous and Al-Anon for more than 60 years and the practice has turned many lives around. Many other groups now use them for a variety of purposes.

We also learn by listening to each other's story in a group setting. If possible, find a support group. Learn as much as you can. Being with others who are also going through a breakup is very helpful and supportive.

AFFIRMATION: Today I will be willing to look for ways to learn as much as I can from this experience.

September 6

Unless we pick up our power and grope our way to adulthood, we will always wait. —Mark Shain

No one can do recovery work for us. Blaming and shaming ourselves, or anyone else, for what went wrong is a waste of time and energy—and keeps us stuck, possibly for years.

When we decide to survive and choose to do what it takes, we act from our own base of power. Will we make mistakes? Almost definitely. Will we fail? Most likely. Will we try again? Yes. Will we continue to improve? We will, if we keep trying. Failing is okay. Being afraid to try is not okay.

AFFIRMATION: Today I will tackle something that has frightened me, and if I fail the first time, I know I can always try again... and again.

September 7

It's not so much how busy you are, but why you are busy. The bee is praised; the mosquito is swatted. —Marie O'Connor

Are we putting our time to good use? As we know, we won't get this day to live again, so we need to make it count. Are we spending our precious time productively, or are we merely keeping ourselves busy without accomplishing much?

The last thing most of us want is to be a nuisance. Are we acting without thinking? Are we trying to do our best before we ask for help? Are we using our resources to annoy someone else? Are we leaning too hard on another person?

Using time productively is taking a giant step toward self-esteem. When we set a goal and work toward it daily, even if only for a little while, we start moving forward and building momentum.

AFFIRMATION: Today I will make an effort to use my time in productive activities.

September 8

Talk doesn't cook rice. —Chinese proverb

Have we been preoccupied and made promises to our children or other loved ones that we haven't kept? We may promise that we'll do something and then put it off. But if we don't deliver, everyone suffers. Others lose faith in us, we feel guilty and defensive and soon lose faith in ourselves.

It's important to our children, particularly in times of transition, for us to be reliable. Let's not make promises we can't keep and make sure to deliver on the ones we do make.

AFFIRMATION: Today I will be careful about what I promise to others.

September 9

Just do it. —Nike slogan

Here's where getting into the habit of listening to one's gut is useful. If we feel strongly that something *needs* to be done—we should do it. Exercise is a good example. We know we should exercise, we know it feels good, we are glad we did it, but still we talk ourselves out of it. I'll do it later; I'm too tired now; I'll do it tomorrow for sure; I'll wait till after.... Whatever. Once we start procrastinating, we can always find more reasons why we shouldn't do something right now.

"Just do it" implies not opening that debate. Don't go there. When you know something is good for you, like having a medical check-up, attending a therapy session, getting to work on time, taking time for the kids—do it! You'll be glad you did.

AFFIRMATION: Today I will look at my resistance to taking action and ask myself "Are my excuses legitimate?"

September 10

Remember, age is not important unless you are a cheese.
—Helen Hayes

It's important not to limit ourselves because of age. People may think they're too old to go back to school, learn about technology or have fun. Others think they're too young to make a difference, or no one will take them seriously.

Age is relative. Just look around and you will see that people of the same age vary greatly in ability and appearance. As long as we are alive, our job is to keep learning and growing. If that stops, we might as well be 120.

AFFIRMATION: Today I will not let my age be a limitation.

September 11

Learn to bend. It's better than breaking. —Leo Buscaglia

Using trees as an analogy, we know that if there are strong roots and the tree is flexible, it can survive the most severe storm. It may lose a branch or two and a bunch of leaves, but it remains standing.

Let your Higher Power be your root system and keep the connection strong. Ask for the strength you need to stay balanced. You will then be able to weather this storm and anything else that comes your way.

Be willing to compromise. Be willing to share. Be willing to do your part to avoid creating further damage to the family system.

AFFIRMATION: Today I will do my best to balance being flexible and getting my needs met.

September 12

I woke up this morning with devout thanksgiving for my friends, old and new. —Ralph Waldo Emerson

Let's take some time today to thank our friends for being in our lives. Expressions of appreciation bless both giver and receiver and most of us don't get enough appreciation on a regular basis. Start a trend.

AFFIRMATION: Today I will thank my friends for contributing to my life.

September 13

You don't sing because you are happy; you are happy because you sing. —William James

Singing is a great way to lift the spirit. It requires use of breath so our lungs get a workout, bringing more oxygen to the brain. Listening to upbeat music can change our mood by itself, but singing along brings the music right into our bodies and elevates the mood even further.

If you don't know the words, use la la la, hum or whistle. If you've been told you can't sing, it's time to sing your heart out. Sing in the shower, sing in the car. Sing hymns, sacred music, rock and roll, opera, country or jazz—whatever you like—and give it everything you've got.

Singing can release your blocks. It might even make you cry. It can move you onto a different level of awareness. It can also awaken your joy. If you really like to sing, you might think about joining a choir or choral group. It's great therapy.

AFFIRMATION: Today I will sing with some music that makes me happy.

September 14

You'll never be the person you can be if pressure, tension, and discipline are taken out of your life. —James G. Bilkey

Isn't this true? As much as we may dislike pressure, tension and discipline, and often have to deal with too much of these, without them would we expand our capabilities? Would we *volunteer* for really hard work and practice self-discipline without any pressure?

We seem to learn and achieve the most when we are challenged. Courage grows, intense self-examination is more likely and a closer connection with a Higher Power is established when we feel threatened. There are no atheists in the foxholes, as an old saying goes. Times of great challenge are often the ones we remember as the major turning points in our lives.

While we, to the extent we can, need to moderate the degree of tension we allow into our lives, it's good to recognize that this force will stretch us into more than we would have been without it. Let's use this time as an opportunity to be more than we have been.

AFFIRMATION: Today I will list all I have learned and accomplished lately and see how much tension and pressure had to do with it.

September 15

The secret to achieving your goals is mental conditioning. Review them at least twice daily. Post your goals where you're sure to see them every day: in your journal, on your desk, in your wallet, or over your bathroom mirror. Remember, whatever you consistently think about and focus upon, you move toward.* This is a simple yet important way to program yourself for success.
—Tony Robbins

This is an extremely effective exercise! Do we want to earn more money, get a new job, have better relationships with our children, write a book, make more friends? Let's write our goals down and look at them often. The more we see them, the more real and achievable they become.

AFFIRMATION: Today I will choose at least one goal for myself, write it down and post it in places where I will see it often. For an extra boost, I will ask my Higher Power to help me with it.

*Note: This statement is also true for negative thoughts (hatred, resentment, vengefulness, etc.), so let's choose our thoughts wisely.

September 16

I held a moment in my hand, brilliant as a star,
fragile as a flower, a shiny sliver out of one hour.
I dropped it carelessly.
O God! I knew not I held an opportunity. —Hazel Lee

As we cope with a crisis, we find ourselves ruminating about the past or worrying about the future. A whole day can go by without us hardly noticing it. This day will never happen again. Our children will never be this exact age again, we will never be this young again, opportunities will be offered that may not be offered again. Let us be alert to the beauty of today.

AFFIRMATION: Today I will stay alert for opportunities to appreciate and enjoy my life.

September 17

One can spend one's whole life climbing the ladder, only to realize it's been placed against the wrong wall. —Joseph Campbell

The idea that we may have been with the wrong person, particularly if the relationship has been a long one, can be very upsetting. We may feel that our love was given in vain; that the time was wasted and would have been better spent with another person. This can be very demoralizing.

Remember that love is never wasted. We learn a lot about ourselves by understanding why we made the choice we made, and by examining our own behavior. Sometimes a relationship teaches us what love *isn't*.

The next step is to understand ourselves very well, so we don't do the same thing again.

AFFIRMATION: Today, instead of feeling discouraged, I'll decide to take a good look at what I may have learned from this relationship.

September 18

He who cannot rest, cannot work;
He who cannot let go, cannot hold on;
He who cannot find footing cannot go forward.
   —Harry Emerson Fosdick

In the early days following a separation it's hard to rest, work and most of all, to let go. Feverish rounds of thinking and rethinking keep us busy. Our attention span is short. Some of us avoid activity and sleep as much as we can.

It's helpful to realize that this is the way our minds begin to cope with a new and difficult situation and we need to take care of ourselves until we feel better. We cannot go forward to find a new orientation for our lives until we have rested and recovered. The amount of recovery time differs with each person and depends on many variables. Let's be patient and gentle with ourselves during this time.

AFFIRMATION: Today I will be gentle and patient with myself.

September 19

One way to become enthusiastic is to look for the plus sign. To make progress in any difficult situation, you have to start with what's right about it and build on that. —Norman Vincent Peale

Enthusiasm is both attractive and contagious. There's usually something good in any situation, if we look for it. Not seeing any good is a sign that we are depressed, which is part of the separation process, particularly if we didn't decide to leave the relationship and would still like it to exist. Feeling sad and blue is a normal response to not having what we want.

When we want to change our state, however, gratitude is the antidote. We can choose to be grateful for one or for many things, and once we do this we feel our mood begin to lighten and become more hopeful. Maybe things aren't as bad as we thought. Maybe blessings are being granted in the midst of the difficulty that we hadn't noticed until now.

AFFIRMATION: Today I will write a list of all the things I'm grateful for. The more I practice this, the more I'll realize the positive aspects of my life.

September 20

I love you —Higher Power

We are never truly alone, unless we believe we are. Have you noticed that those who are connected to the Higher Power, regardless of religion or style, are happy —happier than those who claim God doesn't exist?

Our Higher Power is there for us whether we know it or not but many of us don't utilize the connection. Because we have free will nothing is forced on us, but love surrounds us all the time. We just have to let it in.

Let's extend an invitation to God and ask that this Universal energy come into our lives today. A little willingness is all it takes to start building a relationship with God.

AFFIRMATION: Today, even if I don't believe it will happen, I will invite my Higher Power into my life.

September 21

Worry is the interest paid on trouble before it comes.
  —William R. Inge

When we worry we may suffer twice—once by worrying and again, if and when the incident actually occurs. Most of what we worry about never happens. On the slim chance our worries materialize, we don't want to be worn out in advance by stress.

Worry can also paralyze us. It enlarges our fears and often stops us from doing something we might want or need to do. Let's not dwell in worry or anxiety. We can allow it, acknowledge it and know it's temporary. We might tell ourselves " I know I feel worry but most of what I worry about never happens. If I change my scene or activity level, I'll feel better."

AFFIRMATION: Today I know I'm a capable person and if I need help, I'll find some. This too shall pass.

September 22

There is nothing stable in the world, uproar's your only music.
  —John Keats

Separation from a partner and divorce create a tremendous uproar for sure, in the form of change that swirls around us constantly. If we struggle to keep things unchanged in our lives, we will be fighting a losing battle and will always be unhappy.

Change is good. Change creates fear, but also excitement. If we look at change as negative, we miss opportunity. We all have experienced change that seemed unacceptable, but later discovered it was just what we needed. Let's learn to enjoy the uproar in anticipation of what is to come.

AFFIRMATION: Today I'll let go of the past and welcome today with all it's marvelous potential.

September 23

I am entitled to miracles. —A Course in Miracles

Hard as this is to believe, we are entitled to miracles. We need only to ask for them. We can't control another person but we can ask for skills to cope with a situation. If our partner has left us, we may ask for the ability to let go. If our children are in crisis, we may ask for the grace and wisdom to be good parents. If money is a problem, we may ask for a better job.

We can ask our Higher Power to enter a situation and heal it. The results are amazing. When we ask for help it's important to be alert for the help we receive.

AFFIRMATION: Today I'll ask my Higher Power to enter a situation that's giving me trouble.

September 24

Art is the only way to run away without leaving home.
   —Twyla Tharp

Expressing ourselves through art is absorbing, satisfying and good for our mental and physical health. We don't have to think we're talented to enroll in a class or experiment with an art medium or craft; we just have to be willing to try. Many of us deny ourselves an opportunity for self-expression because we believe we have to be a genius before we even get started. Be willing to be imperfect, to make a mess, to try and fail—that's how we learn. If we keep at it, we'll improve.

There are many varieties of artistic endeavor to choose from: dance, paint, write, carve, draw, sculpt, sing, play an instrument—try one! This may be the time to sign up for a class, find a book or look for a teacher. Art is another area of self-discovery and one that can bring much pleasure to daily life.

AFFIRMATION: Today I'll choose an art form or craft and explore it, or go back to it. I will enjoy the act of creation—without worrying about result or perfection.

September 25

If you can't feed a hundred people then just feed one.
  —God's Little Devotional Book

We all have something we can share. Maybe it's food, money or time. This reminds us that we don't have to be grand to be helpful, just willing. Is there someone you know whom you might invite to dinner? Someone who can use some company?

Doing a service for another person brings us blessings. If someone has been good to us, this is a way of passing the blessing along. Grace enters our lives from doing acts of kindness.

AFFIRMATION: Today I'll pass along an act of kindness to another person.

September 26

Your soul doesn't care what you do for a living—and when your life is over, neither will you. Your soul cares only about what you're being while you're doing whatever you're doing.
  —Neale Donald Walsch

Doing is good and we all need to take action, perform, earn a living and take care of our responsibilities, but we are more than that. As John Bradshaw says, we are human beings, not human doings.

What's the big picture? Who do we want to be? In his book, *The Seven Habits of Highly Effective People*, Stephen Covey suggests that we think about our own funeral and what we'd like people to say about us, and live our lives accordingly. This will define *who* we have been, which is more important than *what* we have been.

AFFIRMATION: Today I will choose an attribute that I'd like to be remembered for and practice it.

September 27

... and they lived happily ever after.

Most of us bought into this storybook ending, which we first heard as children. People fall in love, unite, and that's the end. Happiness is guaranteed, right? If our lives don't follow this pattern, we feel like failures, even though we know it happens to others all the time.

We are very rarely told, at any time in our lives, about how love is a daily decision, that resentments are poison, that having babies may be hard on a relationship, or how we are to cope with major shifts in priorities.

Relationships need constant nourishment if they are to survive, yet how often do we allow work or children to take precedence over the sustenance of our adult relationship? "Happily ever after" doesn't exist for anyone. There are periods of ups and downs in all relationships, and most of us haven't learned the skills we need to cope with the range. Some of us had good examples set by parents, but for many the opposite is true.

Let's decide to learn everything we can about creating successful relationships by talking to people who have good relationships or marriages. We can also read some of the many books on the subject. (See the list at the back of this book.)

AFFIRMATION: Today I'll forgive myself for my part in what went wrong and decide to learn as much as I can to prevent the same mistakes from happening again.

September 28

Creative minds always seem to survive any kind of bad training.
—Anna Freud

Albert Einstein didn't do well in school. The French Impressionists were thought to be thoroughly inadequate.

As children we may have been told that we couldn't sing or that we weren't smart enough. Someone might have said we had two left feet or made fun of a drawing or something else we made. A partner may have criticized our driving, cooking or the way we speak. Let's not allow that to stop us today.

Each one of us is creative in a unique way. There is not one who doesn't have a gift of some kind. The challenge of being human is to uncover it, for God surely put it there.

AFFIRMATION: Today I won't let the criticism I've experienced in the past stop me from expressing myself.

September 29

Patience is a virtue.

We must learn patience in order to achieve serenity and peace. We may ask "When will the pain be gone? When will I feel better? How long will it take to recover?" "When will I meet someone new?" These are all good questions, but there's no easy answer to them. For each of us it will take what it takes, and we need to be patient with ourselves and others.

When there's so much stress in our lives, patience may be in short supply and may manifest itself as road rage, being critical of others, lack of tolerance for different opinions and being short-tempered with our children.

A patient attitude is a choice, and we *can* control it. We can stop and take a few deep breaths, leave the room and take time to cool down. We can ask ourselves, "How important is it?" By learning to be patient under difficult circumstances, we save ourselves the necessity for more apologies later on. We become proactive, rather than reactive.

AFFIRMATION: Today I will practice patience.

September 30

If you always do what you always did, you'll always get what you always got. —Moms Mabley

Repeating behaviors while expecting different results is one definition of insanity. This is a powerful idea. If we want a different result then we have to change something. If we've always been a doormat, it's time to say "No." If we've tried to buy the love of another and it hasn't worked, we need to try a more direct approach. If one tack has been unsuccessful after a number of attempts, it's time to do something different.

Maybe it's time to let go, or stand up for ourselves, or leave a situation. Maybe we need to take action or be patient. Maybe we need to listen to another person's point of view, rather than promote our own side.

This quote contains a powerful idea. Make a change where the same old thing isn't working.

AFFIRMATION: Today I'll see if doing the same thing is preventing me from getting the results I want. If so, I'll choose a different course of action.

October 1

One day at a time. —Alcoholics Anonymous slogan

No matter how daunting the tasks ahead may seem, we only have to take them a day at a time. If our lives seem totally out of control, taking just today and thinking about what we can do in the next few waking hours makes life more manageable. If we want to stop ourselves from doing something, we just have to stop it today—that's all. The present is where our power lies. We may make decisions to change something forever, but today is all that's within our control. One day leads to the next, and if we continue, the new habit will grow just as the old one did.

If we feel down and depressed, we can believe that tomorrow will be different. We just have to get through today. Some of us find it useful to take only an hour or a minute at a time.

AFFIRMATION: Today I won't let myself be overwhelmed. I'll do what I can, knowing that's good enough.

October 2

Recover or repeat. —Twelve Step Divorce Recovery Program

When a long-term significant relationship ends, we need time to recover. Endings create wounds—some more serious than others—depending on the length and depth of the relationship. It's important to understand our role.

If we slam the door on recovery and begin dating right away, we will likely make the same mistakes again. We may choose the wrong person or sabotage a new relationship because we haven't worked through our emotional reaction to the breakup. We will miss the lessons the relationship could have taught us.

Going from one relationship to another, dating only because our former partner is in a relationship, or being very critical of others are signs that we have recovery work to do.

Let's be gentle with ourselves and take time to absorb the lessons and heal our hearts.

AFFIRMATION: Today I'll know I need time to recover. I'll take all the time I need.

October 3

Enjoy simple things.

We can get more out of life by noticing and appreciating the simple things. Sitting outside with a steaming cup of coffee watching the sunrise, enjoying the aromas of baking or cooking, noticing sunlight play across a field or through leaves on a tree, watching a child perform in a school play, listening to favorite music or taking a hike can bring great pleasure.

Let's be alert and enjoy as many moments as we can.

AFFIRMATION: Today by enjoying simple things, I will feel more happiness.

October 4

Security is mostly superstition. It does not exist in nature nor do the children of men as a whole experience it. Avoiding danger is no safer in the long run than outright exposure. Life is either a daring adventure or it is nothing. —Helen Keller

If we wait until we are safe to learn something new or change a behavior, we may wait a very long time to make a move. If we choose security over self-development, we risk our lives in a different way.

Security is an illusion. Some people feel relatively safe working on steel girders or on bridges out in the open, at extreme heights. Some feel safe parachuting out of planes. Others don't feel safe driving a car on an inch of snow, or they worry about speaking in front of a group of people.

Let's expand our definition of security and choose to venture out into new experiences. Let's create adventure!

AFFIRMATION: Today I'll tolerate feeling uncomfortable as I plan something new.

October 5

Everything that irritates us about others can lead us to an understanding of ourselves. —Carl Jung

If we find ourselves becoming very irritated by an aspect of another person, it's because that particular irritating feature is also present or was present in us. Because we aren't able to see ourselves objectively, this is a tool we can utilize for better self-understanding.

For example, if we become annoyed by someone's pettiness, it may be that we are reacting to suspicions of our own pettiness. It's not usually obvious because there are style differences or variations in the degree of the behavior. But if we're reacting to it, we can know that it's present in us too. In a separation, the very thing that's upset us with our partner is also present in us in some form.

AFFIRMATION: Today if I find myself negatively judging another person, I'll see what I can learn about me.

October 6

Never argue with an idiot. They drag you down to their level, then beat you with experience. —Unknown

This bit of humor is a reminder that we must choose our battles wisely. When a major life change occurs and shifts are necessary, people get upset. There will be many opportunities for arguments—with our ex-partner, children, relatives, attorneys, certain friends and co-workers—as we make our way and adjust to the new circumstances.

We need to conserve our energy and go to the mat only on important issues.

AFFIRMATION: Today if I feel the need to defend myself, I'll evaluate whether it's really worth doing or if I can just let it go.

October 7

Say what you mean, but don't say it mean. —Unknown

We can and should express our opinions, but we don't have to beat a person with a club to get our point across. There's a big difference between stating our preferences or views and attacking another person verbally. Demeaning words are very destructive and hurtful. What's more, nothing positive is accomplished by them.

Children are especially affected by meanness. Their self-esteem is diminished when a parent says negative things about who they are. For example, there's a difference between: "You are a bad child" and "I don't like the way you are acting." In times of high stress we need to be very careful of how we speak to people. Monitoring ourselves is our responsibility, regardless of provocation.

AFFIRMATION: Today I will speak from the "I" perspective, stating my opinion or preference without attacking the other person.

October 8

Interdependence is a fundamental law of nature. Many of the smallest insects are social beings who, without any religion, law or education, survive by mutual cooperation based on an innate recognition of their interconnectedness.
—His Holiness the Dalai Lama

Divorce does not eliminate the family, but redefines it. Interconnectedness is still critical for children as well as parents. Family life, when defined by hostility and competitiveness, becomes a living hell for all. When defined by mutual cooperation, family life can re-create itself in a new way where everyone benefits.

Flexibility will be important as children's needs change. Each parent will also require cooperation from the other at times. It's important to be as cooperative as possible because, as we know, what goes around comes around.

AFFIRMATION: Today, and as time goes on, I will be as cooperative as possible.

October 9

Today's mighty oak is just yesterday's nut that held its ground.
—McKinly

If you have a goal to achieve—to learn something new, to be an excellent parent, to make more money, to earn a degree, to find a new place to live— do something every day toward that goal. Don't give up! We can achieve just about anything, if we consistently apply effort day after day.

The mighty oak doesn't grow tall overnight. Most major accomplishments take time, so let's expect that and be patient with ourselves. If we keep a clear picture in mind of what's desired and do something toward it every day—even if it's just making a phone call—at the end of one month, there will be significant gains.

AFFIRMATION: Today I will create a mental picture, or even a drawing, of the goal I have in mind and do something every day to make it a reality. I can make it happen!

October 10

Experience is a good teacher, but her fees are very high.
—Lifeminders.com

We don't have to reinvent the wheel. When it comes to relationships, separating from a partner, divorce, recovery, figuring out what to do and not to do, there is plenty of information available. We can avoid many mistakes by listening to the advice and experience of others. We can read, talk to others who are positive role models, attend support groups or see a therapist. We might attend a parenting class for divorcing or separating parents. Taking advantage of others' expertise will save us worry, time and money in the future.

Each relationship is different, so the conditions of the separation will vary, but there is much to be gained by seeking information and adapting it to our own situation. We don't have to learn everything the hard way.

AFFIRMATION: Today I'll make a list of where I can gather additional information so I can avoid mistakes others have already made. This will put me ahead of the game.

October 11

It's hard to detect good luck—it looks like something you've earned. —Fred A. Clark

"Boy, that person is really lucky, " we might think as we see an actor make it big. We are unaware of the years spent studying and the rejection he endured in the audition process before getting his break. We see a family of adolescents or young adults who are high functioning and lovely people and we may think "Those parents are really lucky, their kids are great," underestimating the amount of time and energy their parents devoted to raising them.

The good news is that most of the time, luck has little to do with success, so we can get the good breaks too, if we are out there doing all we can to make it happen.

AFFIRMATION: Today I'll work on myself so I can be "lucky" too.

October 12

Every day we should reach out and touch someone. We all love the human touch and most of us get too little of it. A warm hug, a touch on the arm or a pat on the back is good for both the giver and receiver.

Loss of touch is particularly difficult after a separation. Some of us seek it in places that aren't good for us. Hugging a friend is often soothing and helps us feel connected again. Hugging our children is wonderful for all concerned.

Massage therapy is another safe way to be touched and has other therapeutic benefits as well, like improved circulation, loosening of tight muscles and general relaxation.

AFFIRMATION: Today as I go through my day, I'll look for appropriate opportunities to use touch in a loving way.

October 13

Lord, either lighten my burden or strengthen my back.
    —Thomas Fuller

Surviving the loss of a relationship is overwhelming at times. The impact is felt in many areas of our lives, and on some days we may feel like we'll never get over it.

Prayer is good for times like these. There's nothing wrong with calling for reinforcement. A Higher Power is the best ally we can have as we face the challenges of a new and sometimes painful situation. When we ask, help will be given.

AFFIRMATION: Today I will remember to ask my Higher Power for help and to appreciate it when it comes.

October 14

Adversity causes some of us to break, others to break records.
—William Arthur Ward

We choose our reaction to adversity. Will we allow challenge to break us or will we take it on, do our best and become stronger than we were before?

Some of us will never get over the breakup. We might become bitter and depressed and choose not to create a new life. We may cling to the old ways and refuse to move on.

Some of us, in spite of enormous odds, come back better than ever. Some start new careers, others connect with people they never would have met and enjoy activities together. Some of us attempt and achieve more than we ever thought possible.

The choice is ours—will we sink or swim?

AFFIRMATION: Today I realize that my attitude about my situation will either make or break me.

October 15

We make a living by what we get, but we make a life by what we give.
—Winston Churchill

If we find ourselves alone as we face a separation, volunteering is a wonderful way to connect with people. There are many ways to do this—through an organization, a house of worship or on our own.

As children we love to receive, but as adults we learn that it's giving that is the most pleasurable. Helping another person who is needier than we are warms our hearts and connects us with others. Surely someone we know can use a hand today.

AFFIRMATION: Today I will look at my immediate circle of family and friends and decide who might need some attention from me.

October 16

Hope begins in the dark, the stubborn hope that if you just show up and try to do the right thing, the dawn will come. You wait and watch and work. You don't give up. —Anne Lamott

Hope is such an important thing. When we're feeling sad and lonely, we may feel like giving up. We may believe we'll never be happy again or we'll never find another relationship like the one we had.

We do go on. We will survive. If we act as Lamott suggests— show up and do the right thing, wait, watch and work—we will see that our lives work out and in time may be better than ever.

Don't give up. If we find ourselves really depressed and hope is hard to find, see a therapist. There are many ways to treat depression today, and no one has to suffer indefinitely any more.

AFFIRMATION: Today I will show up and do the right thing.

October 17

We must be the change we wish to see in the world.
—Mahatma Gandhi

If we want people to be fair with us, we have to be fair. If we want generosity from others, we must be generous. If we want our children to respect us, we must respect them. If we want others to care about us, we must be a caring person.

Whatever we may want from another, we need to be that first.

AFFIRMATION: Today I will give to others what I want most.

October 18

Some [people] wait for something to change and nothing does change so they change themselves. —Audre Lord

This quote is the essence of the Twelve Step programs. Our only power lies in what we do and think; yet these are very powerful. The job we want may require more education than we have. We may not be able to change that, but we can go back to school. Our world may be far from perfect, but we can make a contribution somewhere to improve life for one person. Others may tell lies about us, but we can live in a way so they won't be believed.

We create our world by the way we think, the actions we take and those we avoid. When we become frustrated by a person or situation and are unable to change it, we need to change ourselves.

AFFIRMATION: Today I will examine a situation where I believe I have no control. I will ask myself if there is a way I can change it by changing me or by altering my perception.

October 19

There is never a wrong time to do the right thing.
   —H. Jackson Brown, Jr.

During the ending of a relationship, we are tempted many times to do the wrong thing. Some of us think that this is the time to make demands, to lie about what is needed, to say we don't have enough. People say mean things to their children about the other parent and unknowingly cause their children great suffering. Do we want this for ourselves and our family?

As we make the global decision to do the right thing, our lives improve. Even if others choose differently, we can still take the high road. This course of action pays enormous dividends that we may not be able to see in the moment.

AFFIRMATION: Today I will do the right thing and be an excellent role model for my children and others.

October 20

Press on. Nothing in the world can take the place of persistence. Talent will not; nothing is more common than unsuccessful men with talent. Genius will not; unrewarded genius is almost a proverb. Education alone will not; the world is full of educated derelicts. Persistence and determination alone are omnipotent.
—Calvin Coolidge

Is there a dream to be created? Is there a goal to work toward? What is it that would really be worth achieving? For each of us the answer is different, but we all have a dream for ourselves. Maybe it's just to survive this breakup.

Coolidge's statement is full of hope because we don't have to be a genius, great looking or a Rhodes Scholar to achieve our dreams. We only have to set the goal and keep moving toward it. Setbacks will occur; that's to be expected. It may take longer than we originally thought, but it's only time. Time passes whether or not we are making progress, so we might as well use the time in a way that will enhance our lives. We must not give up!

AFFIRMATION: Today I'll press on in the direction of my goal.

October 21

Remember, a closed mouth gathers no foot. —Steve Post

When in doubt about whether to speak, give advice or yell at someone, the best course is to say nothing. It's easy to fool ourselves into thinking we know what's best for another person, but often we don't. Less said, less mended, as wise proverb goes.

When we feel generally upset, we may be tempted to overreact. Avoid this by waiting and thinking first. Let's take some time, walk away, breathe and examine the situation carefully.

AFFIRMATION: Today I'll practice listening carefully before I speak.

October 22

Consider the postage stamp: its usefulness consists in the ability to stick to one thing till it gets there. —Josh Billings

When life is chaotic and there's so much to be done, our efforts may become scattered, so that we're working hard and racing around, but not accomplishing much. This kind of activity is buying into an *illusion* of busyness, and the results can be frustrating and disappointing.

This is a good time to stop, think and prioritize. Choose one thing and stick with it until it's finished. It may seem like we're not doing as much, but the end results are usually solid. Make your environment as pleasant as you can while you work. For example, play some music in the background, have a cup of tea or a cool drink, wear comfortable clothes. Be good to yourself and give yourself a little reward as you complete each task.

AFFIRMATION: Today I'll establish my priorities, evaluate them in order of importance and get to work. I'll take on one project and stay with it until it's finished. If I can't finish it today, I'll come back to it tomorrow.

October 23

It's only possible to live happily ever after on a day-to-day basis. —Margaret Bonnano

Expecting "happily ever after" from a relationship is lunacy. Relationships are hard work. To maintain one we need to examine our beliefs and our behaviors, be willing to compromise, to communicate and tolerate, to adjust, and to be mature enough to keep a relationship alive. Making sacrifices doesn't always make us happy.

Making the decision to do these things on a day-to-day basis produces a good relationship, which may be one ingredient in our happiness. Deciding to be positive and grateful daily enhances happiness. Having work that we love—or deciding to love our work— will make daily life better.

Choosing our attitude each day will determine our happiness.

AFFIRMATION: Today I'll be happy.

October 24

Courage is grace under pressure. —Ernest Hemingway

It takes courage to do something we've never done before, or to go to court to argue for our needs and the needs of our children. It takes courage to leave an abusive relationship or to stand up for ourselves. It takes courage to live on our own. It takes courage to learn new skills, go to job interviews—to face life on our own.

The good news is we can pray for courage and grace, and it will be given to us to get through whatever we need to do. Courage is feeling scared and doing it anyway, but we don't have to do it alone.

AFFIRMATION: Today if I'm feeling scared, I'll ask my Higher Power to help me be courageous.

October 25

An obstinate man does not hold opinions—they hold him.
  —Samuel Butler

Flexibility is a great trait to cultivate. When we get locked into a stance and can't deviate an inch in either direction, we are in trouble.

A wise person examines her or his own beliefs and opinions in the light of new information and makes adjustments. This does not suggest allowing ourselves to be bullied, but only to be flexible in our thinking. Let's be open to options and compromise and be willing to search for the win-win solution.

AFFIRMATION: Today I'll evaluate whether I'm being obstinate in any current situation.

October 26

You will never "find" time for anything. If you want time you must make it. —Charles Baxton

The Seven Habits of Highly Effective People by Stephen R. Covey is a great book for learning how to create time for important things. Although we all lead busy lives, there is usually more time available than we think. We may have to give something up or utilize hours differently but managing our time is an important skill to learn.

For example, getting up an hour or two earlier may help us get some quiet, private time to concentrate. A writer, who was also a full-time salesperson, wrote a book from 6 to 8 a.m. Others may work better late at night, after everyone else is in bed.

We may also need to make time to take care of ourselves. We all need rejuvenation, and if we don't have some rest and relaxation, the effects will create health problems later. Balance is the key word in effective time management.

AFFIRMATION: Today I'll make some time to evaluate how I *use* my time.

October 27

For time will teach thee soon the truth. There are no birds in last year's nest. —Henry W. Longfellow

We may worry that our ex-spouse will say things that turn our children against us. Maybe we are concerned about the structure we have to create and the discipline that we as parents need to provide while the other parent has fun with the kids. Maybe unkind things are being said about us among our friends. This feels bad, and we may wonder what we can do to stop it.

If we continue to live our lives with integrity and honesty, the truth will eventually become clear. Lies and manipulation also become obvious. Situations that were once confusing usually right themselves in time. In contrast, when we engage in retaliation and escalate the drama, all involved look very unattractive. The main idea is to monitor our own actions and be sure that when the truth does come out, we smell like a rose.

AFFIRMATION: Today I will make sure that I act with honesty and integrity, regardless of temptation.

October 28

It's so simple to be wise. Just think of something stupid to say, then say the opposite. —Sam Levenson

It's so important to keep our sense of humor. Laughing is good for us and is a wonderful relief from the seriousness of the situation.

Go to the humor section in a bookstore and read a few pages. Be with people who make you laugh. You might want to let them know that laughing is what you need. Be silly and sing funny songs. If you have children, do this with them. Adolescents will be totally horrified, but it's good for them to see their parent feeling happy. Our children worry about us when we're sad.

Even though we may feel awful at times, we can always take a break and do something to lighten up. We needn't make feeling down a full-time job.

AFFIRMATION: Today I will get a few laughs in, because it's good for my body, mind and spirit.

October 29

Be ready at all times for the gifts of God, and always for new ones.
   —Meister Eckhart

To be ready to receive—to have faith that the gifts will come—is a form of mastery. To *know* that God grants grace, help and abundance and to be grateful in advance, is a sign of faith. Faith is rewarded.

AFFIRMATION: Today I will ask for the help I need and wait with a grateful heart for my answer.

October 30

Today I am nourished and supported by positive thoughts. I choose my thoughts as I do my friends, staying with those I find uplifting.
—Hazelden Thought for the Day

Are we aware that our thoughts create our perception of reality? At first this idea may seem ludicrous, but it is true that our experience is shaped by our thoughts. For example, take a rainy day. We may think that it's dreary and a nuisance, or we may choose to think that we need the rain and that it makes us feel cozy when we're indoors. We may enjoy the sound of it as it hits the roof or window. It's all a matter of perspective.

AFFIRMATION: Today I choose to nourish myself with positive thoughts.

October 31

Get a life in which you are not alone. Find people you love, and who love you. And remember that love is not leisure, it is work.
—Anna Quindlen

Some of us relied mostly on our partners to make social connections so after a separation, we may find ourselves feeling very alone. This may create the temptation to find another partner to fill the void. Before moving into another relationship, there's recovery work to do. We must grieve, detach from the former relationship, determine who we are now and what we need. If left undone, this will undermine any new relationship.

Instead, we can get a life and foster friendships. We may connect more closely with our siblings, get in touch with people we haven't seen in a long time, and make the effort to stay in touch with current friends. We can join a support group, a church group, an activity group and meet new friends. It takes work, but the effort pays off.

Romantic relationships may come and go, but if we have the loving support of friends and family, we won't feel desperate and alone. We are better able to determine if a romantic relationship is good for us if we are strong rather than needy.

AFFIRMATION: Today I will put some effort toward creating a firm foundation of support by cultivating relationships with friends and family. I will also support them when they need me.

November 1

One definition of insanity is thinking we know what the other person is thinking and responding to that without verification.

When we assume we know what another person is thinking, we risk major misunderstandings. This is especially true during emotional upheaval, where perspective and emotions are likely to shift often.

Our reaction to what we *thought* we heard may surprise and confuse the other person. He or she then responds to our reaction, and the whole exchange may be totally based on an inaccurate understanding of each person's point of view.

The moral of the story is not to assume we know for sure. Ask and clarify the other person's perspective before taking action. One way to do this is to repeat what we heard the other person say and ask "Is this right?"

AFFIRMATION: Today I will clarify the other person's point of view before saying or doing something I may regret.

November 2

Separation from a long-time partner creates a wound on psychic and emotional levels. The longer the relationship, the deeper the wound.

To achieve full healing from psychological and emotional trauma, we need to give ourselves time—to grieve, to learn to live alone again, to experience our individuality, to assess and recover from any damage done to us by the relationship itself, and to evaluate and absorb the lessons offered by the relationship.

Every relationship teaches us something. Some teach us what to do, and others what not to do. Most are a combination of both, and this assessment is important to our evolution. This is an important step toward creating healthy relationships in the future.

For parents: Children need reassurance and recovery time too. They need extra attention and reassurance, as if they were getting over an illness.

AFFIRMATION: Today I will consciously give myself time to work on my recovery.

November 3

People ask, "Aren't you dating yet? You need to get on with your life," as if I don't have a life already.

Well-meaning people ask this without realizing how demeaning it can be. Do we believe that if we aren't part of a couple we don't have a life? Individuality is encouraged in the United States. We drive our own cars, choose our jobs, practice a religion or not, dress the way we want, and enjoy many more individual freedoms. Yet as adults we are often expected to be part of a couple, and a heterosexual couple at that. Our married friends may not be able to see the value of being single.

There's nothing wrong with being single. It's empowering for us to learn how to live on our own. In fact, after living with a partner for many years, it's essential to be alone, at least for a while. We need to teach ourselves to be strong and independent.

Independence doesn't come overnight, but it does happen when we give ourselves the time and patience to develop it.

For parents: Children need time to adjust to the loss of a parent in their home. If we wait to date until the children feel secure in the new situation, they will be better able to cope with new people in their lives.

AFFIRMATION: Today I realize that it's perfectly acceptable, and even liberating, to be single. I need time, and so do my children.

November 4

The only time you don't fail is the last time you try anything—and it works. —William Strong

Don't be afraid of failure. Think how many times inventors attempt an idea before it works. Artists paint over a canvas to remove what they don't like or start a new one. Writers throw away many pages before they are satisfied with a manuscript. Their editors suggest that they throw out even more, or maybe start again. People who weren't good students in school often turn out to be very successful when they find their niche later on. We may not be good at one sport but find we do well at another.

Let's be willing to fail and still persevere. Let's be willing to change, tweak and mold an idea until it's developed. If the idea doesn't work out, it's not because *we* are failures, it's because *the* idea didn't work out. There are many more where that came from.

For parents: Children need to be able to try and fail too. If they are criticized too often, they will stop stretching. Encouragement and brainstorming are good actions for parents.

AFFIRMATION: Today I won't be afraid to fail. In fact, I'll welcome it, because it shows that I'm moving forward.

November 5

I walk in gratitude today.

If we're having a bad day, we may resist this idea, but let's suspend our resistance and try it. Let's be grateful for everything with which we come in contact.

Let's look around. Right now, in this moment, are we okay? Are we better than we were a while ago? Is there food in the refrigerator? Do we sleep on a bed?

As we go outside today, do we see a blue sky, or cloud formations or feel the rain on our faces? Is there the lively energy of a city around us or the serenity of the countryside? Are there trees and birds or other animals around? Do we have a job and make a living? Do we have children to be proud of? Do we have skills? How about friends who support us?

When we have this focus, joy comes. Try it—all day.

AFFIRMATION: Today I will be grateful for everyone and everything I meet.

November 6

Have you ever noticed? Anybody going slower than you is an idiot, and anyone going faster than you is a maniac. —Jerry Seinfeld

We tend to judge people by where we are and how we feel in the moment. It's important to recognize that our perceptions may be biased.

AFFIRMATION: Today I will pay attention to my negative judgments and realize they may be colored by my state of mind.

November 7

Persistence overshadows even talent as the most valuable resource in shaping the quality of life. After all, no one ever achieved a goal by being interested in its achievement; one must be committed. Isn't it possible that short-term "failures" may actually provide you with the necessary insights or distinctions to create even greater success in the future?
—Tony Robbins

As we build a new life and learn how to cope on our own, persistence is necessary. Building a new skill usually requires tolerance for not feeling in control and being less than an expert with the new task for a while. It takes time to learn something new. Mistakes are inevitable, and unless we are willing to make them, we'll be stuck where we are.

AFFIRMATION: Today I will go easy on myself as I create my new life. I will allow myself to make mistakes in order to learn new skills.

November 8

Our unconscious is like a vast subterranean factory with intricate machinery that is never idle, where work goes on day and night from the time we are born until the moment of our death.
—James Harvey Robinson

We are constantly thinking and processing— information, emotions, fears, dreams, judgments of ourselves and others—in the factory of our unconscious mind. Our unconscious mind speaks to our conscious mind, and the talk can be positive or negative.

When we were children, many of us were told that we were naughty or bad. We may have been told we drove people crazy, we were not good or smart enough, or we didn't deserve good things.

These messages may still reside in our unconscious mind, and we may say these things in our self-talk. We may think "Good things never happen to me," or "How could I do that, I'm so stupid!" or "I deserve whatever happens to me."

Whenever we catch ourselves thinking negative thoughts or making negative statements to ourselves, we can STOP and replace the negatives with positives: "I am a good person"; "I deserve to be happy"; "Abundance flows in my life." If we stop the negative self-talk, it will make a difference.

AFFIRMATION: Today I will not beat myself up. I will replace negative thoughts with positive affirmations.

November 9

Miracles are occurring all around us every day, and sometimes the miracle is that something does NOT occur, or it may be something that we don't even stop to notice. —Joan Levin

We may have wanted something very badly, prayed for it, wished for it, hoped that God would grant us this favor and still not received it. Later on we may realize something better was waiting for us. Someday, we may actually be grateful we didn't receive what we thought would be good for us. God's answer may have been "Not now, my child, I have something much better in mind for you. Be patient a little longer."

Sometimes we're answered and we don't notice it. Maybe we prayed for help and someone came along and gave us a hand. We may think help has to appear a certain way and miss the fact that our prayers were answered after all.

God works through us. He sends us to each other. Let's be willing to give and receive through our fellow human beings and even our pets.

AFFIRMATION: Today I will watch for miracles.

November 10

Both partners feel alone when they separate but the person who is separated from the children feels more alone. —Bob Givone

In the support groups we suggest that people wait awhile before they date. We need to take time to examine what happened and adjust to the separation before we rush out the door.

When we are busy with children, it's easier to take this pause. With kids in the house, we are not truly alone. While the need to connect with other adults is strong, it's not as strong as it is for the person who is used to living with his or her family and is now on their own.

It's critical, especially in the early stages of separation, to find support and connection with others. This is different than dating, which can be daunting, confusing and ultimately adds to a sense of loneliness if it's begun too early. There are many non-romantic ways to connect with others and by taking this action, we lessen feelings of depression and isolation.

On the other hand, the person who is the custodial parent has most of the parenting responsibility, which is always challenging and even more difficult when it was previously shared. Neither side of the story is easy and everyone needs support.

AFFIRMATION: Today I will have compassion for myself and for my former partner, realizing it's not easy for either of us.

November 11

The nightingale gets no prize at the poultry show. —Sir Walter Raleigh

If we aren't accepted the way we are, it may not be because there's something wrong with us—but instead, there's something right!

AFFIRMATION: Today I understand that if I don't fit in where I used to, it's not because there's something wrong with me.

November 12

There is only one courage and that is the courage to go on dying to the past, not to collect it, not to accumulate it, not to cling to it. We all cling to the past, and because we cling to the past we become unavailable to the present. —Osho

The present is where our personal power resides. Right now. This instant. The constant, present moment is always opening to us. When we reside in the past, we miss our creative moments. One by one they go by. The same is true for worrying about the future.

Learning from the past is good. Spending all of our time in that mode is disempowering.

AFFIRMATION: Today I will let go of the past and start creating a full and happy life for myself.

November 13

You never....
You always...

These two expressions are communication killers. We all use them, but because most of the time they are untrue, it voids whatever statement follows them.

"Always" and "never" are absolutes. Human beings are rarely *always* or *never* anything. We communicate more clearly when we avoid these kinds of statements.

AFFIRMATION: Today I will remove the words "always" and "never" from my communication style.

November 14

Problems are opportunities in work clothes. —Henry Kaiser

Our attitudes about problems are what color our lives. If we think our problems are worse than anyone else's and complain at every opportunity, we create a bleak outlook on life.

If we look at problems as challenges and opportunities to learn valuable lessons, our outlook will be sunnier. Yes, problems take us out of our comfort zone and push us to do more, but they also offer opportunities to demonstrate our abilities, to learn new material and give us life experience. From these experiences, we gain confidence and become more and more competent.

AFFIRMATION: Today I will look at my problems as valuable learning opportunities, realizing even if unwanted or challenging, they increase competency.

November 15

Happiness makes up in height what it lacks in length. —Robert Frost

We all know that life has its ups and downs. One way to lengthen the upswings is to recognize, relish and remember them. The more we are grateful for happiness and the good things that come our way, the more we will recognize them. The more we are aware of our blessings, the happier we will be.

One of the downsides of a split or divorce is that because we are so upset, we may not notice the good things going on around us. If we don't notice the goodies, we may perceive a totally bleak picture, which is rarely the truth, and this perception will likely increase or deepen depression. We can make happiness last longer by practicing gratitude.

AFFIRMATION: Today I will lengthen the good times by being grateful for them.

November 16

If you keep your mind sufficiently open, people will throw a lot of rubbish into it. —William A. Orton

Let's be careful about whom we listen to and ask for advice. There are some folks who relish talking negatively about people like a dog loves to gnaw on a bone. They are always ready to help fan the flames. There are others who will exacerbate fear by telling us every horror story they know about other peoples' divorces or splits. Some will criticize us and talk about what we should have done differently.

Instead, let's choose people who will listen or give sound advice. Maybe there are people who live in a way we'd like to emulate. Let's use them as role models and gather wisdom and ideas from their example.

AFFIRMATION: Today I will evaluate those I confide in carefully, making sure I choose sound and healthy people.

November 17

Just for today, I will be agreeable. I will look as well as I can, dress becomingly, talk low, act courteously, criticize not one bit, not find fault with anything, and not try to improve or regulate anybody except myself. —Ruth Carter-Bourdon

All of these suggestions are actions we can take or changes we can make. We know that when we take the time to look really nice, we feel better. When we live and let live, we are more serene. When we say nice things to others, our spirits are lifted too.

If we are tempted to criticize, we might ask ourselves, "How important is it?" Do we really have to say it? Hearing criticism sucks the energy out of us, no matter who we are. Wouldn't we like to hear positive comments instead?

AFFIRMATION: Today I will be agreeable.

November 18

Do not deny what you feel, but keep in the back of your mind that it will pass.—Iyanla Vanzant

In the early days of separation, we may wonder whether we will survive. The pain is intense. We may have headaches, stomach problems, feel feverish, numb, confused, unable to concentrate, depressed, worried and more. The good news is this will pass, and more quickly when we have support. As we learn to adapt, the symptoms diminish, clarity and understanding increase, and we do go on.

It's helpful to remember that many people have been through this pain, have survived, and in time have created wonderful new lives. Through time and self-examination, we will get there too.

AFFIRMATION: Today I will keep in mind that there are better times coming.

November 19

No snowflake in an avalanche ever feels responsible.
—Stanislaus Lezcynski

Everyone has some responsibility for the demise of his or her relationship. We were like a snowflake each time we chose not to be loving, criticized or failed to appreciate our partner. This metaphor may also be applied to relationships with our children. One snowflake may represent a failure to set a limit or when we allowed inappropriate or unloving behavior.

Let's assess the role we play in our relationships and realize that it's the little things we do or don't do which create the big picture.

AFFIRMATION: Today I will seek to understand my responsibility in the ending of this relationship so I won't continue to make the same mistakes.

November 20

Ninety percent of the friction of daily life is caused by the wrong tone of voice. —God's Little Instruction Book

When we are upset it usually shows in our voices, and often before we even realize it. A harsh tone of voice can make a person feel ashamed, intimidated, accused or demoralized, to name a few. The use of sarcasm is another variation of negative tone and is particularly hurtful to children. Or we may even say nice things, but when a harsh tone is used we still give a negative message.

When feeling defensive and afraid, it's important to monitor our tone of voice so we don't exacerbate a situation—particularly if there are children involved. If necessary, we can take a break, walk away for a bit and calm down, and resume communication when emotions are under control.

AFFIRMATION: Today I will monitor my tone of voice and observe the reaction of others.

November 21

Authentic success is being so grateful for the many blessings bestowed upon you and yours that you can share your portion with others. — Sarah Ban Breathnach

There is nothing like being of service to others to get us out of the doldrums. When we give of ourselves, in time or in material things, we are uplifted. It is natural that when we extend love, love is returned. We don't know from where, but it will be returned.

Gratitude for our blessings assures more blessings. Positives attract positives and negatives attract negatives so the more positive we are, the more positives we will see.

AFFIRMATION: Today, even if I'm feeling sad, I will appreciate all the blessings of my life.

November 22

May the food we are eating make us aware of the interconnections be-
tween the universe and us, the earth and us, and all other living species
and us. Because each bite contains in itself the life of the sun and the
earth, may we see the meaning and value of life from these precious mor-
sels of food. —Thich Nhat Hanh

We are fortunate indeed if our plates are full. Let's be thankful for
all the elements and preparation that brought our food to our ta-
ble. One meal represents the work of many people, the lives of
animals, the soil, the rain and seed. All are indeed connected. Let
us be grateful.

AFFIRMATION: Today, as I eat a meal, I will be conscious and
grateful.

November 23

Offer grace for the bounty of goodness. Raise the song of harvest home,
the glass of good cheer, the heart overflowing with joy. We have so much
for which to be thankful. So much about which to smile, so much to
share. So much, that in this season of plenty, we can embrace the season
of relinquishment. All we have is all we need. —Sarah Ban Breathnach

Holidays are difficult, especially in the first year following the
end of an important relationship. We need to be prepared to create new traditions to celebrate, to do something different to make
the tradition unique and enjoyable this year.

Call a person who is lonely. Volunteer in a soup kitchen for
the homeless. Write a gratitude list with your children. Making
plans in advance helps us get through the holiday season with
less fear and pain. Don't wait to be invited, arrange something
yourself.

AFFIRMATION: Today I will start a new holiday tradition.

November 24

When we consciously choose growth over stagnation and fear, the divine spirit of the universe will support our decision by bringing us our lessons gently and lovingly.—Iyanla Vanzant

We have choices—we can choose personal growth and learn as much as possible from our situation, or we can hold on to the past and when that doesn't work, become bitter. If we choose growth, we will be led in that direction. If we choose stagnation, we will experience the obstacles that accompany negative beliefs. When in doubt, let's choose growth.

AFFIRMATION: Today I choose to learn, grow and become more conscious as a result of my experience.

November 25

In every person who comes near you look for what is good and strong; honor that; try to imitate it, and your faults will drop off like dead leaves when their time comes. –John Ruskin

We all incorporate positive and negative traits. No one is perfect. There are a few who have almost no redeeming features and a few who are 99 percent good, but most of us are somewhere in the middle. Every person, including a child, has a lesson to teach. Let's be open to the lessons offered by others.

AFFIRMATION: Today I will expand my experience by paying better attention to every person I meet.

November 26

When we do the best we can, we never know what miracle is wrought in our life or in the life of another. —Helen Keller

We can't be perfect, totally brilliant and compassionate, or completely organized at any one time, but even less during a separation. We can only do the best we can. Taking the high road, not acting on thoughts of revenge or avoiding meanness will stretch us to our limits some days, but will also bring us peace in the long run.

If every day we do our best, we will see good adjustments being made, growth occurring and we'll be a great example for our children.

AFFIRMATION: Today I will give my best effort, without expecting perfection from myself.

November 27

I live in the present. I can courageously handle anything as long as I take it one moment at a time. This too shall pass.
—Sue Patton Theole

A lot of the fear we experience comes from projecting too far ahead. We look at what must be accomplished and feel totally overwhelmed by the enormity of it. We can shut down completely if we do this. If instead we think about only the next single step—getting dressed, brushing our teeth, making a phone call, doing some research, writing a note, having some lunch—we can keep fear at bay.

When we project far into the future before we've done the groundwork, of course it seems overwhelming. By taking life a day or even a moment at a time, we'll build a foundation for the solution to unfold and we won't become paralyzed. Seasickness can be prevented by eating small amounts frequently and likewise, fear can be reduced by taking one small step after another, until we reach our goal.

AFFIRMATION: Today I will not allow myself to become overwhelmed. I will take it a day or a moment at a time until I reach my goal.

November 28

The act of sharing ourselves with others by giving, is another way of increasing our self-worth. —Susan Fautwasser

Our self-esteem suffers during a breakup. If we are the one who left the relationship, we probably feel guilt and perhaps like a bad person. If we were the one who was left, we may feel worthless or undeserving. During the transition into single life, our self-esteem may ebb and flow like the tide.

In the early days, we may be too fragile to reach out to others, but after a while we will see that we are able to help those who are struggling. We have more compassion because of our experience. By extending ourselves to others, we come to appreciate what the experience has taught us.

Members of divorce support groups help each other. Some people serve in soup kitchens during the holidays; others organize toy collections or coat drives. These activities, and those like them, take us out of ourselves and broaden our views. As always, helping others helps us too.

AFFIRMATION: Today I will look for opportunities to share myself.

November 29

People who work for the Dalai Lama believe that when a lot of things start going wrong all at once, it is to protect something big and lovely that is trying to get itself born—and that this something needs for you to be distracted so that it can be born as perfectly as possible. —Anne Lamott

A lesson in the Course in Miracles workbook states: "I don't know what anything is for."

We have all had the experience of living through an awful time only to find out later that it led us to something we wouldn't have found without the original series of events.

Faith is knowing that, even in the midst of calamity, good news is coming. There is a reason life unfolded this way.

AFFIRMATION: Today I will be open to the idea that something big and lovely is trying to be born.

November 30

You are goodness and mercy and compassion and understanding. You are peace and joy and light. You are forgiveness and patience, strength and courage, a helper in the time of need, a comforter in time of sorrow, a healer in time of injury, a teacher in times of confusion. You are the deepest wisdom and the highest truth; the greatest peace and the grandest love. You are these things. And in moments of your life you have known yourself as these things. — Neale Donald Walsch

Self-centeredness is a hallmark of divorce, but we can choose to be different. Not only will defining ourselves as goodness, mercy and compassion make us feel good, but it will have wonderful results in all areas of our lives. When we choose our actions rather than react, we create for the future a life that's full and happy and we become marvelous examples for others.

Whom would you rather spend time with—a person who has the attributes listed above or someone who is self-absorbed?

AFFIRMATION: Today I will choose to embody at least one of these attributes.

December 1

The hardest thing of all is learning to be a well of affection, and not a fountain, to show them that we love them, not when we feel like it, but when they do. —Nan Fairbrother

Parenting during a separation or divorce is a major challenge. We become the only parent at home when the children are with us. We may be in pain, depressed, angry, frightened or worried. Yet our children depend on us to be responsible, supportive and mature.

As this quote suggests, we need to allow our children, and others as well, to have the choice of private time or contact with us. We have our "well of affection" ready but wait for appropriate times to show it. This is attending to their needs, not our neediness. This is an important distinction.

AFFIRMATION: Today I will create my well of affection and have it available when my children or others need it from me.

December 2

The secret of life is not to get rid of the butterflies in your stomach but to get them to fly in formation. — Unknown

We will rarely be confident about everything. We will almost always have "butterflies" about something, so if we wait until we get rid of that feeling, we won't move at all.

We need to manage the fear and move ahead.

AFFIRMATION: Today I'll manage my anxieties and do what I have to do.

December 3

A man who studieth revenge keeps his own wounds green.
— Francis Bacon

It's tempting at times to seek revenge for what has been done to us, but exacting revenge keeps us in darkness. We can't move on or be happy until we let this desire go.

Revenge may take the form of turning children against their other parent, failing to adhere to agreements, saying "No" when we can say "Yes," playing mind games or telling lies about the other person.

Let's keep in mind that what we put out comes back, and that revenge can be an endless cycle that destroys everything in its path.

AFFIRMATION: Today, although I may have occasional thoughts of revenge, I don't have to act on them. I'll put my energy to better use.

December 4

Do not be too timid and squeamish about your actions. All life is an experiment. —Francis Bacon

We won't know until we try, and try we must! During this period, we will be called upon to do things that we haven't done in a long time, or perhaps never before. If we look at life as an experiment, we will understand that only some of what we attempt will work. We'll learn from our mistakes and do better the next time. This is how life advances.

AFFIRMATION: Today I will go for it and not be hard on myself if I don't get it right the first time.

December 5

Everybody comes from the same source. If you hate another human being, you're hating a part of yourself. —Elvis Presley

When we find ourselves reacting strongly to another person, it's generally because the trait that's triggering our response is also present in us. It may not take the same form or be less than obvious, but it's worth thinking about in depth.

When we identify and correct this characteristic in ourselves, we will no longer be triggered by that behavior in someone else.

AFFIRMATION: Today I recognize that if I feel hate or disgust toward someone, I need to look into myself for the reason.

December 6

Age doesn't always bring wisdom. Sometimes it comes alone.
—Unknown

Since we have to go through this difficult time, let's at least gain some wisdom in the process. What might we become aware of, learn, experience, grow from, change, improve? What will we be able to teach others?

Wisdom usually comes from applying knowledge to, and experimenting with, challenges. We don't seem to gain much insight when everything is going smoothly so let's make the most of this mayhem and learn what we can.

AFFIRMATION: Today I recognize that I'm growing wiser and stronger because of my experience.

December 7

Every time you don't follow your inner guidance, you feel a loss of energy, a loss of power, a sense of spiritual deadness.
—Shakti Gawain

How many times have we had a strong feeling that we should or shouldn't do something, but didn't pay attention to it? We went along with others or talked ourselves out of it. We paid more attention to our minds than our gut feelings and later regretted it.

Inner guidance is often the best source of information. It may defy logic and not be what everyone else is thinking, but let's not forget to add our intuition to the other sources of information we are considering.

AFFIRMATION: Today I'll meditate and add my inner guidance to my resources.

December 8

Peace is not something you wish for; it's something you make, something you do, something you are and something you give away.—Robert Fulghum

To young people peace is not a priority. In fact, during adolescence and in our twenties, being peaceful may seem like being bored.

As we get older and have more responsibility, the concept of peace becomes more attractive. Being peaceful means sleeping at night, suffering less anxiety, having patience or being gentle with our children and ourselves.

It may mean being considerate about when and how we say things, being flexible in our dealings with others and listening to a friend when he or she is upset.

So if peace is our goal, we must be active about achieving it. It's worth the trouble. Who would we rather spend time with—a person who is frantic or usually upset about something, or someone who is serene and gentle and leaves us feeling better than before?

AFFIRMATION: Today I will create more peace in my life.

December 9

Every blade of grass has its angel that bends over it and whispers, "Grow, grow." —The Talmud

We are on a journey while on the earth, and it's the quality of the journey, not the destination, that counts in the end.

At the end of our life, where we lived, how much money we had, how many degrees we earned or how physically attractive we were is not what matters. The quality of our relationships is what's most important. How did we treat the people we loved—the children we raised, our mates, family members and friends? How did we relate to our co-workers and the merchants, friends and strangers who presented themselves?

We are placed on the earth to expand our awareness and to learn to love one another. We have been given the means to do that. We just have to ask God to help us blossom in this way and we will see or feel the support that's all around us. Spiritual help isn't forced on us; we have to invite it and allow it to enter.

AFFIRMATION: Today I'll visualize an angel who is helping and encouraging me to evolve.

December 10

People are only mean when they are threatened.
  —Morrie Schwartz

We may be generous and kind most of the time, but may find ourselves jumping to conclusions, snapping at people or reacting harshly because of the stress inherent in a breakup. We feel vulnerable during times of change and so do the other family members. Let's do what we can to be gentle and reassuring whenever we can.

AFFIRMATION: Today, if someone is mean to me, I will think about the possibility that I may be threatening him or her. I'll choose a different way to communicate in order to foster peace between us.

December 11

Nothing makes you realize you don't know what you want more than getting what you want. —Jane Wagner

When our relationship has been over for some time, we may long to be in another relationship. We may believe that being with someone new is exactly what we need, and we may have ideas about who and what that person should be. If those ideas are based on what we thought was good when we last dated, the criteria may no longer apply. A current assessment of who we are now and what kind of person is right for us today is appropriate.

Being alone is better than being in a bad relationship. What most of us realize eventually is that unless we have worked through the issues from the last relationship and have spent some time by ourselves, it feels uncomfortable to be in a new one.

AFFIRMATION: Today I will be gentle with myself and give myself plenty of time to recover.

December 12

Diamonds are only lumps of coal that stuck to their jobs
  —B. C. Forbes

When we have been rejected we may feel like lumps of coal that aren't worth very much. Our self-esteem plunges, and we may wonder if we will ever feel good and worthwhile again.

In spite of this we gradually become able to take care of our daily responsibilities, do our best to be good parents and do our jobs well. We develop strength of character, resolve and endurance. We stretch farther and do so under more difficult personal circumstances, than we ever thought possible.

As we become stronger, more compassionate and capable than before, our inner grace and wisdom begin to show and we shine, reflecting the glow of our internal process.

AFFIRMATION: Today, in spite of this trial and because of it, I will become even more of a gem than I am now.

December 13

Simplicity is the most difficult thing to secure in this world; it is the last limit of experience and the last effort of genius.
  —George Sand

When it comes to sorting out possessions, less is more. There is freedom in unloading and unburdening ourselves. The ego may fight for what is rightfully ours, but let's keep asking ourselves "How important is it?"

In the end, it may be that the fewer things we have to worry about, the richer our life becomes.

AFFIRMATION: Today I will keep it simple.

December 14

With kindness, love and compassion, with this feeling that is the essence of brotherhood, sisterhood, one will have inner peace. This compassionate feeling is the basis for inner peace.
—His Holiness the Dalai Lama

When we are locked in combat with another, we have no inner peace. There is tension in the body and mind. Typically divorce means combat, and the fight is with a person we once loved and perhaps still do. It's a very painful and confusing situation.

To return to inner peace, we need to ask our Higher Power to show us how to feel kindness toward, and compassion for, those with whom we struggle. If we can reach inner peace, everything else will be affected in a positive way.

AFFIRMATION: Today I will ask my Higher Power to guide me to a place of inner peace.

December 15

All growth is a leap in the dark, a spontaneous unpremeditated act without the benefit of experience. —Henry Miller

As we leave a long-term marriage or relationship, we will be challenged by new demands and expectations. We will have to stretch beyond ourselves to fill the roles our partner may have played. Each time we do something new, our anxiety erupts: What if I can't? What if I blow it? What happens if I fail?

Growth requires a leap. This can be frightening and exhilarating at the same time. The effort may exhaust us, but we will be happy and pleased with ourselves. As we attempt new or forgotten tasks and succeed, we are pushed forward. We begin a positive roll, conquering more and more fear.

AFFIRMATION: Today I will get ready to take the next leap.

December 16

Dare to be yourself. —André Gide

This is the biggest challenge of all. First, we must discover who we really are right now. What's important? How much are we willing to give? What will we tolerate? What do we want? What makes us feel good? What satisfies us?

Then we must live it. We must be true to ourselves and not be dissuaded by the opinions of others. Being genuine takes tremendous courage and involves risks, but living our lives to please others and complying with certain standards that don't feel real to us, is like being only half alive.

AFFIRMATION: Today I will reflect on the times when I feel most connected to who I am and on the times when I feel bent out of shape.

December 17

Life is like a camel: you can make it do anything except back up.
  —Marceline Cox

Once we incorporate new awareness—of ourselves, our relationships, other people, our shortcomings and other types of insights—we can't go back to the old ways. Once we have expanded our views, we can't put Jack back in the box. After a separation, if we decide to reconcile, it's impossible to go back to the old relationship. A new relationship has to be created, acknowledging and incorporating what has happened in the interim.

If we have regrets about the past, we can't change that but we can change our behavior from today onward. It pays to understand our history as much as we can; but then we need to work in the present, which is where our ability to change lies.

AFFIRMATION: Today I will think about my future and do something toward making it as bright as possible.

December 18

Those who attempt to hold on to the past sign up for a lifetime of frustration.

We may wish things were the same as they were and resist the new circumstances. We may deny the present truth, hoping that what once was will be again. We may refuse to work toward acceptance of the new situation.

This is a natural response for a while, but refusing to move on denies us our future. We will remain disappointed and frustrated.

Even if we don't believe it's possible, let's act *as if* we have a wonderful future ahead of us. Let's pretend that we will be and do more than we ever thought we could. If we pretend often enough, we will begin to move ahead.

AFFIRMATION: Today I will act as if I am just fine in my new life. I am calm, competent and creative. I see many new opportunities on the horizon.

December 19

Now I pray that each and every being's true nature be revealed, that we each see clearly our inherent truth and find liberation from the shackles of suffering and difficulty imposed by the limitations of our mind. — Chagdud Tulku

When we were very young, we were taught that many things were dangerous or bad because, as small and vulnerable beings with limited judgment, children need to be protected. Some of those teachings are still with us today, even though they may no longer apply.

Some of us have been taught to suffer, to hold on to grievances, to act like a victim in the wake of someone's words or behavior. This may be socially acceptable and even expected, but doing so is not in our best interest. We suffer when we say to ourselves, "This bad thing will surely happen," "No one loves me or cares about me" or "Oh my God, he or she said.... or did.... and it's so unfair."

If we have to go through the painful ending of a relationship, let's at least learn as much as we can and increase our capabilities. Let's look for new possibilities, different perspectives, expanded spirituality, more knowledge. By these pursuits, we will find liberation from suffering because we will discover how limitless we are. There is no end to the possibilities for personal growth.

AFFIRMATION: Today I choose not to suffer.

December 20

To be in a relationship, interdependence is the way, not independence or dependency.

Independence is highly prized in our society. When we say that someone is "very independent," it's usually meant as a compliment. We imply that the person can take care of him- or herself and isn't influenced by outside pressure.

We may use dependency to describe children who need our care or needy people who seek fulfillment from others. Those who can't stand to be alone and need to be in a relationship to survive are considered dependent, or co-dependent.

Interdependence is an ingredient in most healthy relationships where two independent people choose to share their lives and relate to one another. They don't *have* to be in relationship—they are okay on their own. They *choose* to be together.

Paradoxically, we can't be part of a healthy, interdependent relationship until we become independent. This is where our recovery work comes in. If we become involved in a new relationship immediately after a breakup, we won't re-establish ourselves as independent people. We then attempt to transfer our dependency onto the next person. If we choose a partner from a dependent position, we tend to repeat our mistakes.

AFFIRMATION: Today I will think about the degree of my independence, so that when the time comes, I can be part of a healthy, interdependent relationship.

December 21

In the depth of winter, I finally learned that there was within me an invincible summer. —Albert Camus

Surviving a difficult time takes us from the feeling of deep winter to one of spring. When we realize that not only have we made it through, but we've learned, grown and expanded, we bask in the warmth of the summer sun. This is something to be proud of.

This invincible summer feeling will be with us from now on because we've earned it.

AFFIRMATION: Today I know that eventually I will find the summer sun within me, and from now on I know I can survive.

December 22

In real love you want the other person's good. In romantic love you want the other person. —Margaret Anderson

A good indication of whether we want the other person's good is if we will let them go if we know *we* are willing to let them go.

Sometimes we seek to replace our partner or spouse without looking at the issues that destroyed our previous relationship. We haven't examined our shortcomings or responsibility and haven't yet learned from mistakes. We are seeking salve for our wounds and not thinking about the impact that our needs have on the other person. Real love requires self-knowledge and honesty, and if we haven't reached that place, we need to be clear about it.

AFFIRMATION: Today I will evaluate whether I am really ready for a new relationship.

December 23

[Gratitude] can turn a meal into a feast, a house into a home, a stranger into a friend. It turns problems into gifts, failures into successes, the unexpected into perfect timing, and mistakes into important events.— Melody Beattie

Becoming grateful is the way to happiness. As we're all aware, there are always problems to deal with, but often at least 50 percent of our lives may be going well, yet we choose to focus on the down side much more than it deserves.

Beattie's quote suggests that we look at events differently and reframe them in a positive context. This is not to deny their reality but to expand it. There are many gifts to be received from this practice.

AFFIRMATION: Today I will search for *something* positive in any situation I perceive as negative.

December 24

This holiday season start a new tradition.

Due to tradition, the sentimentality of Norman Rockwell paintings and the extensive marketing that begins in October, holidays take on a larger-than-life aspect, and it's easy to lose a healthy perspective. A holiday is one day. Twenty-four hours pass, and it's over. We can cope with anything for twenty-four hours.

When we find the holidays particularly difficult, it's essential to take special care of ourselves. We might buy ourselves a present, invite friends to decorate the tree or share a meal. Most children love to have company at home and delight in helping with the preparations. It doesn't have to be fancy, and others may contribute to the "feast." If we can't be with family, we can create a family of friends who also may be alone.

There are many ways to celebrate, and this is an opportunity to do something different. Don't wait to be invited—make plans. We may also discover that a new tradition is better than an old one.

AFFIRMATION: Today I will be proactive and creative about my holiday plans.

December 25

The winds of grace are blowing all the time. You have only to raise your sail. — Ramakrishna

"The winds of grace" is a euphemism for God. If we raise our sails and show a little willingness, we will be rewarded. Grace is all around us whether or not we are aware of it, so why not allow that wonderful, empowering, healing energy into our lives?

AFFIRMATION: Today I will raise my sail so that I too will be in the flow of grace.

December 26

Would you rather be right or happy? — A Course in Miracles

The need to be right comes from the ego. The effort it takes to prove that we are smarter, better, holier or wiser than another person often makes us tense and edgy. There may be a perverse pleasure in this pursuit but it is usually short-lived. Sadly, we diminish rather than enhance our relationships by doing this.

Stating our opinion is important. If our perspective is deemed incomplete or wrong, we can accept new information and move on. If we know our opinion is valid, we can calmly restate it and stop there. Letting go and accepting that others have their own perspective frees our minds for more important endeavors.

AFFIRMATION: Today I'll let go of having to be right.

December 27

Don't carry a grudge. While you're carrying a grudge, the other guy is out dancing. —Buddy Hackett

Carrying a grudge literally weighs us down. We may think that by staying angry and resentful we are hurting the person who has caused us anguish. But the other person is rarely aware of how badly we feel or that we may still be reliving and resenting his or her transgression.

If we hold a grudge, we voluntarily continue to live and relive the negative experience. By doing this we give the offender too much power. Let's go dancing instead.

AFFIRMATION: Today I will not allow anyone to rent space in my head.

December 28

It would be possible to describe everything scientifically, but it would make no sense; to would be without meaning, as if you described a Beethoven symphony as a variation of wave pressure. —Albert Einstein

Some of us look for scientific proof that there is a Higher Power and never find enough evidence to satisfy our criteria that one exists. Others know in their bones and beyond all doubt that a power greater than ourselves exists, is accessible and resides within us.

As always, we have a choice about what we believe. Wouldn't it be reassuring to believe that there is a loving Presence nearby to comfort and support us whenever we call for help?

AFFIRMATION: Today I will meditate on the possibility of the presence of God.

December 29

I'll lean on you and you lean on me and we'll be okay.
  —Dave Matthews Band

This is an important time to connect with others. Separation from a significant other or a marital partner creates a feeling of isolation and of being lost. Becoming a member of a support group and meeting other single people, who are either going through or have been through this experience, help enormously. We can check local churches to see if there are any groups in our area. It's very helpful to make new social connections and to talk things over with people who understand.

This doesn't suggest pursuing a romantic relationship right away but making new friends, who in the long run often outlast dating relationships. Friends provide stability when the dating phase begins.

Those who have an active social life and have fun are less likely to become romantically involved out of neediness, or before they are ready.

AFFIRMATION: Today I will look into joining a support group to connect me with others.

December 30

He that cannot forgive others, breaks the bridge over which he himself must pass if he would ever reach heaven; for everyone has need to be forgiven. —George Herbert

Forgiveness is indeed a bridge to peace and serenity. When we hold on to resentment we hold on to pain, and the bridge to peace is broken.

We do the best we can. Sometimes our best is not very good, but it still may be our best given the circumstances. This realization allows us to forgive others. We come to realize that we don't all have the same abilities, tolerances, deficits and strengths. We are unique.

Being forgiven is a blessing. The act of forgiveness doesn't imply that we condone what the other person did but that we can put it behind us, letting go of resentment. Releasing negative energy frees us to live our lives in freedom and peace.

AFFIRMATION: Today, if I am feeling resentment toward another person, I'll think about what it may take to forgive him or her.

December 31

With malice toward none, with charity for all, with firmness in the right, as God gives us to see the right, let us...achieve and cherish a just and lasting peace among ourselves, and with all nations. —Abraham Lincoln

Achieve and cherish a just and lasting peace among ourselves —what a worthy goal. When we achieve peace, we will have far fewer stress-related health problems, we will feel calmer, our minds will be clearer. Besides ourselves, the major beneficiaries of our peacefulness will be our children, in so many ways. If conflict is reduced and we are able to work cooperatively as parents, children do well.

If there is no peace for us yet, we might ask our Higher Power to show us how to move closer toward that goal. Instead of expecting other people to be just, let's focus on what we can do, or stop doing, to encourage peace.

AFFIRMATION: Today I will take an inventory of my thoughts and behavior to analyze whether or not I am contributing to a just and peaceful state.

Bibliography

A Course In Miracles. Triburon, CA: Foundation for Inner Peace, 1975.

Albom, Mitch. *Tuesdays with Morrie*. New York: Doubleday, 1997.

Bach, Richard. *Illusions: The Adventures of a Reluctant Messiah*. New York: Dell, 1977.

Ban Breathnach, Sarah. *Simple Abundance: A Day Book of Comfort and Joy*. New York: Warner Books, 1995.

Beattie, Melody. *The Language of Letting Go*. New York: Harper Collins, 1990.

Buscaglia, Leo F. Loving Each Other: The Challenge of Human Relationships. New York: Fawcett Books, 1990.

Carlson, Richard. *Don't Sweat the Small Stuff...and It's All Small Stuff*. New York: Hyperion, 1997.

Carlson, Richard. *Don't Sweat the Small Stuff at Work: Simple Ways to Minimize Stress and Conflict While Bringing Out the Best in Yourself and Others*. New York: Hyperion, 1998.

Campbell, Joseph, Bill Moyers. *The Power of the Myth*. New York: Bantam Books, 1991.

Chopra, Deepak. *The Seven Spiritual Laws of Success: A Practical Guide to the Fulfillment of Your Dreams*. San Rafael: New World Library, 1994.

Covey, Stephen R. *The Seven Habits of Highly Effective People*. New York: Fireside Books, Simon and Schuster, 1990.

Dass, Ram. *Still Here: Embracing Aging, Changing and Dying*. New York: Riverhead Books, 2000.

Frankl, Viktor E. *Man's Search for Meaning* New York: Simon and Schuster, 1959.

Hahn, Thich Nhat. *Peace is Every Step: The Path of Mindfulness in Everyday Life*. New York: Bantam, 1991.

God's Little Devotional Book for Women. Tulsa: Honor Books, 1996.

God's Little Devotional Book on Success. Tulsa: Honor Books, 1997.

Hay, Louise. *You Can Heal Your Life*. Santa Monica, CA: Hay House, 1984.

Oriah Mountain Dreamer. *The Invitation* San Francisco: Harper, 1999.

Pine, Arthur, Houston, Julie. *One Door Closes, Another Door Opens: Turning Your Setbacks into Comebacks*. New York: Delacorte Press, 1993.

Robbins, Anthony. *Giant Steps*. New York: Fireside, 1994.

Robbins, Anthony. *Personal Power II: The Driving Force*. Robbins Research International, Inc. 1996.

Tagore, Rabindranath. *Fruit Gathering*. Asia Book Corp of America, 1985.

Rodegast, Pat and Judith Stanton. *Emmanuel's Book*. New York: Bantam Books, 1987.

Thoele, Sue Patton. *The Woman's Book of Courage: Meditations for Empowerment and Peace of Mind*. Berkeley: Conari Press, 1996.

Thoreau, Henry David. *Walden*. 1854. Current Edition: Philadelphia: Running Press, 1990

Vanzant, Iyanla. *One Day My Soul Just Opened Up*. New York: Fireside, 1998.

Walsch, Neale Donald. *Conversations with God: An Uncommon Dialogue, Book 1:* New York: G.P. Putnam's Sons, 1996.

Williamson, Marianne. *A Return to Love*. New York: Harper Perennial, 1993.

Kabat-Zinn, Jon. *Wherever You Go There You Are Mindfulness Meditation in Everyday Life*. New York: Hyperion, 1994.

Index

Champion Press, Ltd.
visit our web site to learn more about our
products, receive free newsletters and read
excerpts.

www.championpress.com

Micki McWade maintains a

Thought of the Day

E-mail Newsletter which can inspire, uplift
and encourage you on your journey

to subscribe, visit
www.championpress.com

click on "Authors"
and then on "Micki McWade"